MAX AXIOM
AND THE SOCIETY OF SUPER SCIENTISTS

ANIMAL EXTINCTION
EMERGENCY

WRITTEN BY **EMILY SOHN**
ILLUSTRATED BY **EDUARDO GARCIA**
COVER ART BY **ERIK DOESCHER**

CAPSTONE PRESS
a capstone imprint

Published by Capstone Press, an imprint of Capstone.
1710 Roe Crest Drive
North Mankato, Minnesota 56003
capstonepub.com

Library of Congress Cataloging-in-Publication Data
Names: Sohn, Emily, author. | Garcia, Eduardo, 1970 August 31– illustrator.
Title: Animal extinction emergency : a Max Axiom super scientist adventure / by Emily Sohn ; illustrated by Eduardo Garcia.
Description: North Mankato, Minnesota : Capstone Press, [2022] | Series: Max Axiom and the society of super scientists | Includes bibliographical references and index. | Audience: Ages 8–11 | Audience: Grades 4–6
Identifiers: LCCN 2021012658 (print) | LCCN 2021012659 (ebook) | ISBN 9781663907431 (hardcover) | ISBN 9781663921710 (paperback) | ISBN 9781663907400 (ebook PDF) | ISBN 9781663907424 (kindle edition)
Subjects: LCSH: Extinct animals—Juvenile literature. | Endangered species—Juvenile literature. | Extinct animals—Comic books, strips, etc.
Classification: LCC QL88 .S64 2022 (print) | LCC QL88 (ebook) | DDC 591.68—dc23
LC record available at https://lccn.loc.gov/2021012658
LC ebook record available at https://lccn.loc.gov/2021012659

Summary: Countless animals around the world are in danger of dying out! But why are species going extinct, and how can we protect them? In this nonfiction graphic novel, Max Axiom and the Society of Super Scientists go on an exciting, fact-filled mission to find out.

Editorial Credits
Editors: Abby Huff and Aaron Sautter; Designer: Brann Garvey; Media Researcher: Svetlana Zhurkin; Production Specialist: Laura Manthe

All internet sites appearing in back matter were available and accurate when this book was sent to press.

Printed in the United States 5038

TABLE OF CONTENTS

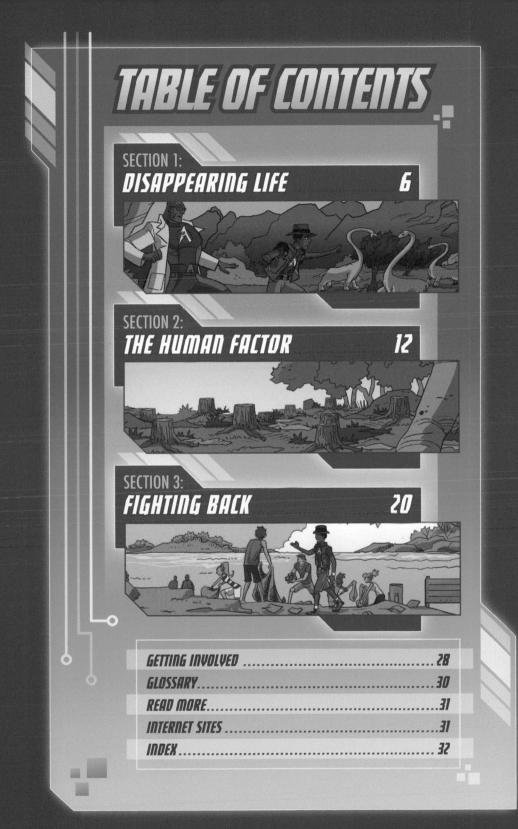

THE SOCIETY OF SUPER SCIENTISTS

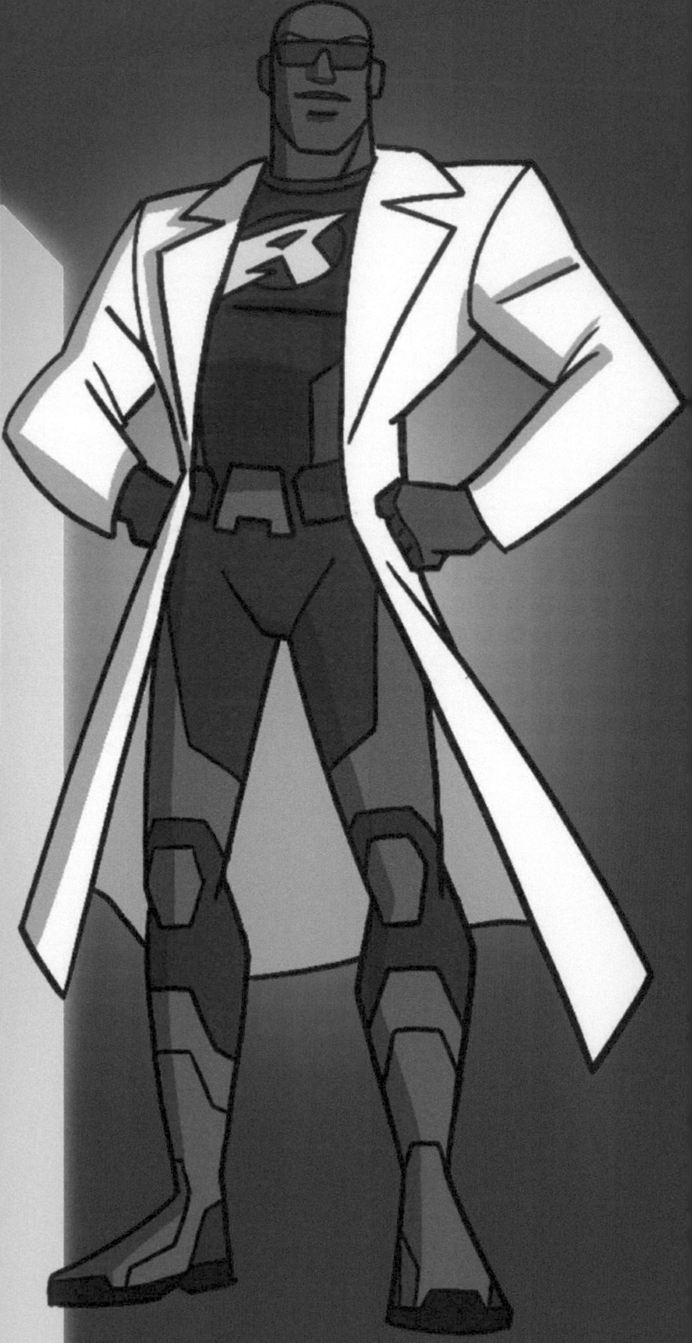

MAX AXIOM

After years of study, Max Axiom, the world's first Super Scientist, knew the mysteries of the universe were too vast for one person alone to uncover. So Max created the Society of Super Scientists! Using their superpowers and super-smarts, this talented group investigates today's most urgent scientific and environmental issues and learns about actions everyone can take to solve them.

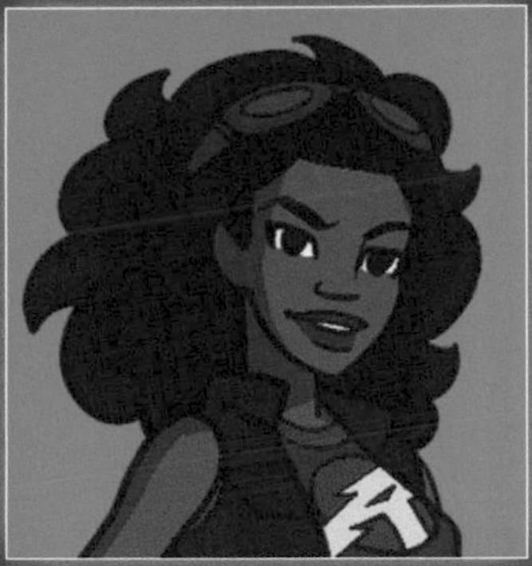

LIZZY AXIOM

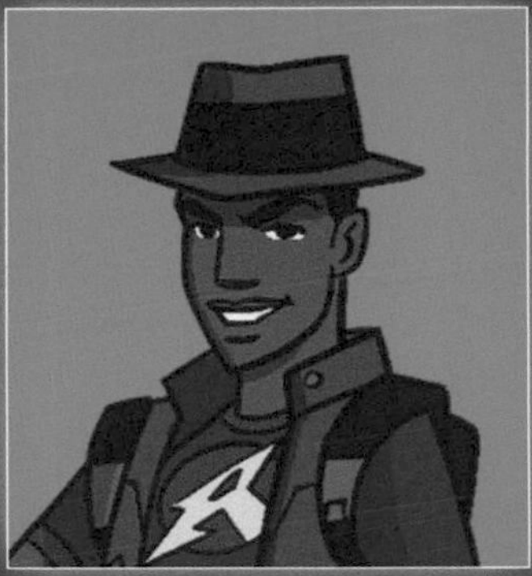

NICK AXIOM

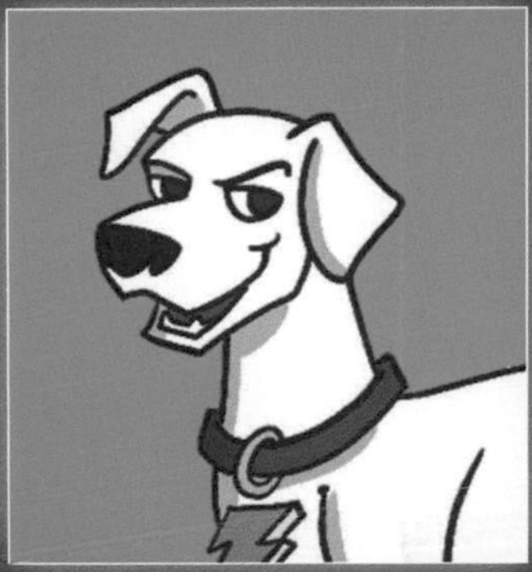

SPARK

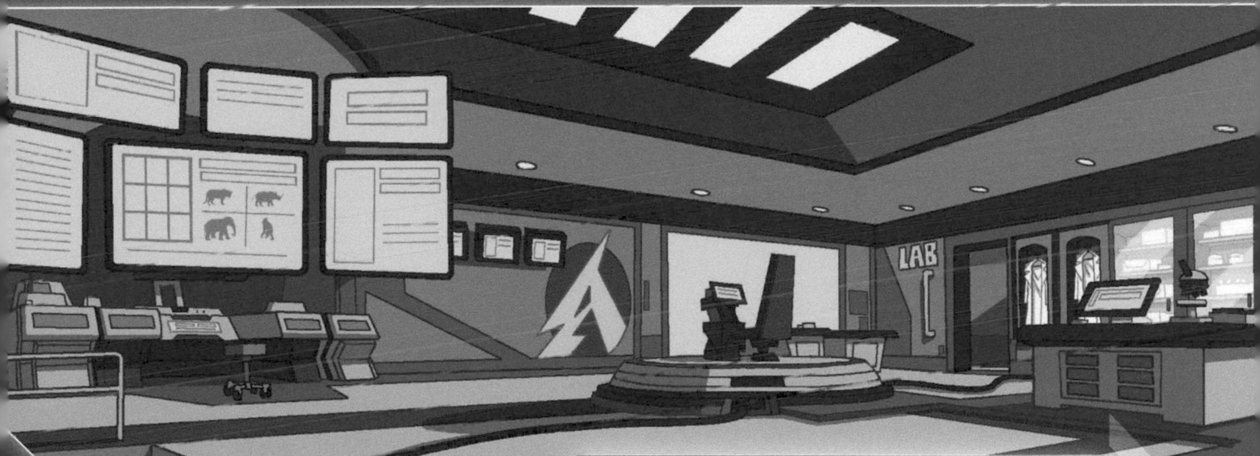
LAB

THE DISCOVERY LAB

Home of the Society of Super Scientists, this state-of-the-art lab houses advanced tools for cutting-edge research and radical scientific innovation. More importantly, it is a space for Super Scientists to collaborate and share knowledge as they work together to tackle any challenge.

SECTION 1: *DISAPPEARING LIFE*

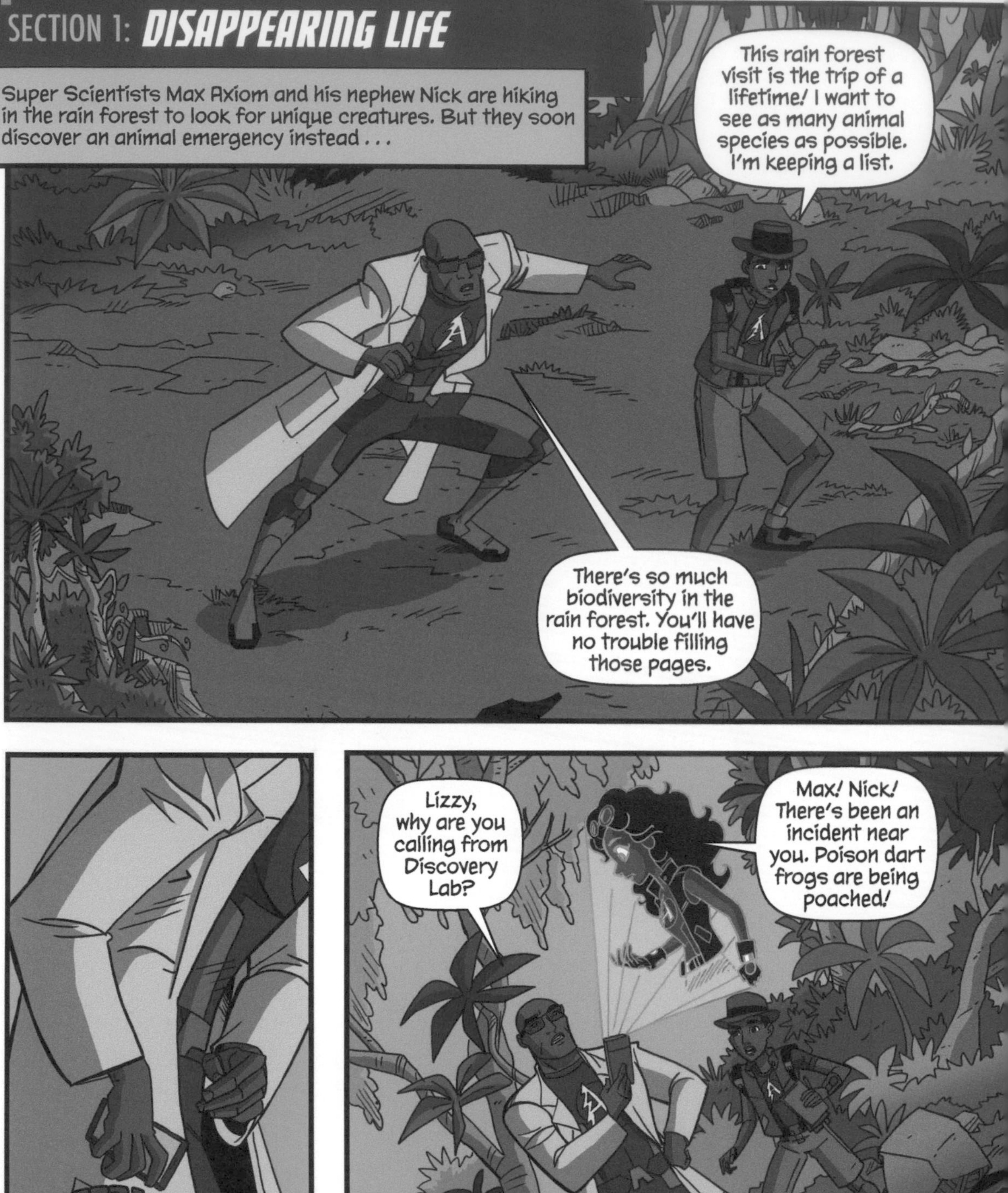

Super Scientists Max Axiom and his nephew Nick are hiking in the rain forest to look for unique creatures. But they soon discover an animal emergency instead . . .
This rain forest visit is the trip of a lifetime! I want to see as many animal species as possible. I'm keeping a list.
There's so much biodiversity in the rain forest. You'll have no trouble filling those pages.
BZZZ! BZZZZZ!
Lizzy, why are you calling from Discovery Lab?
Max! Nick! There's been an incident near you. Poison dart frogs are being poached!

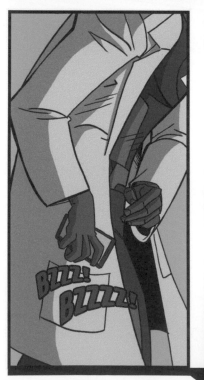

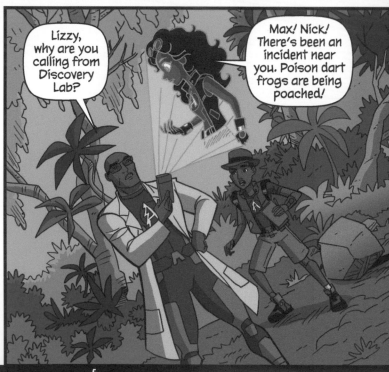

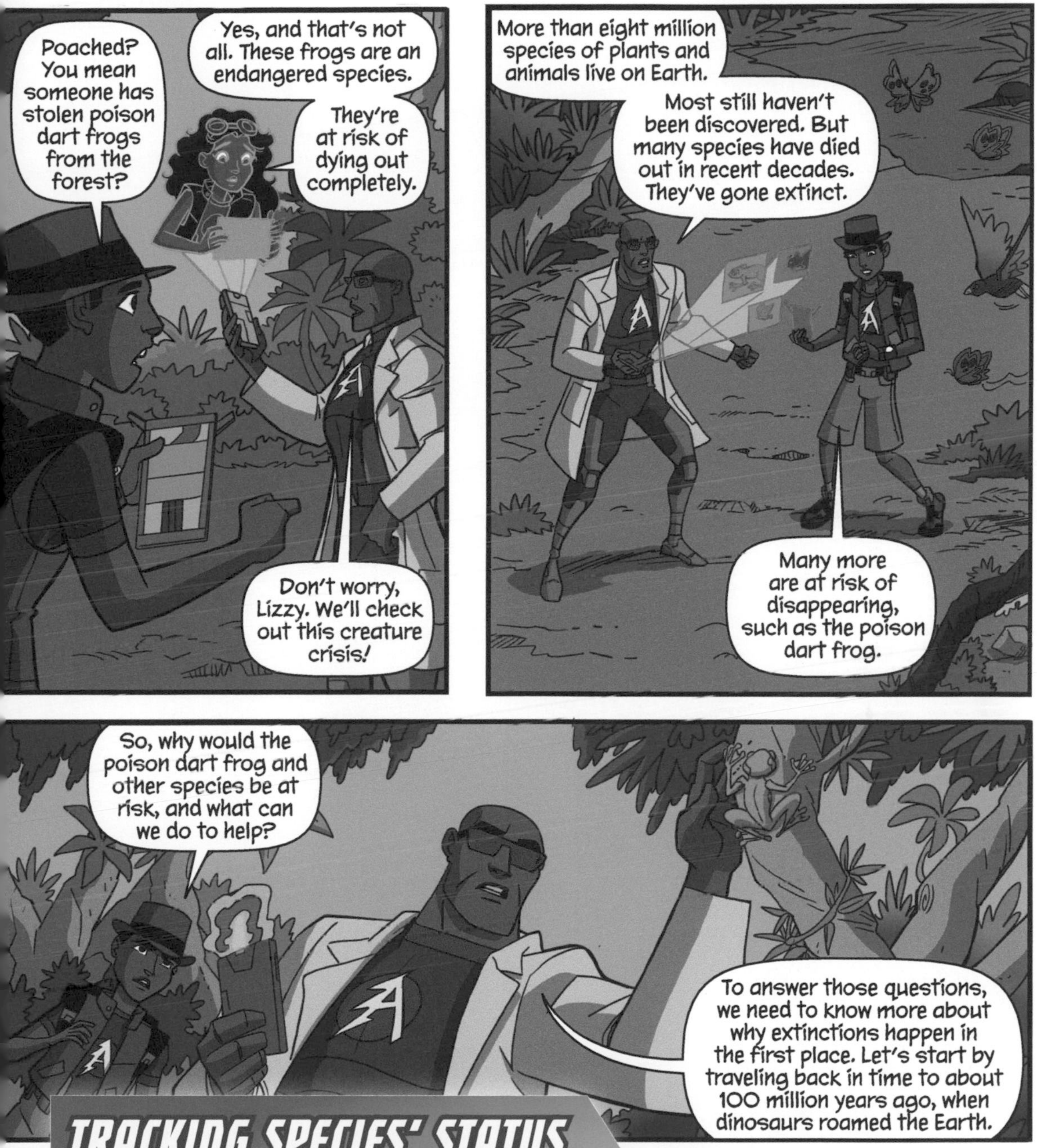
Poached? You mean someone has stolen poison dart frogs from the forest?
Yes, and that's not all. These frogs are an endangered species.
They're at risk of dying out completely.
Don't worry, Lizzy. We'll check out this creature crisis!
More than eight million species of plants and animals live on Earth.
Most still haven't been discovered. But many species have died out in recent decades. They've gone extinct.
Many more are at risk of disappearing, such as the poison dart frog.
So, why would the poison dart frog and other species be at risk, and what can we do to help?
To answer those questions, we need to know more about why extinctions happen in the first place. Let's start by traveling back in time to about 100 million years ago, when dinosaurs roamed the Earth.

TRACKING SPECIES' STATUS

The International Union for Conservation of Nature (IUCN) keeps track of how species are doing. The IUCN Red List is the official source of their status. There are nine categories. On one end are extinct and extinct in the wild (but still living in protected places). Then comes critically endangered, endangered, vulnerable, near threatened, and least concern. The last two categories, data deficient and not evaluated, are used to list species for which too little information is known.

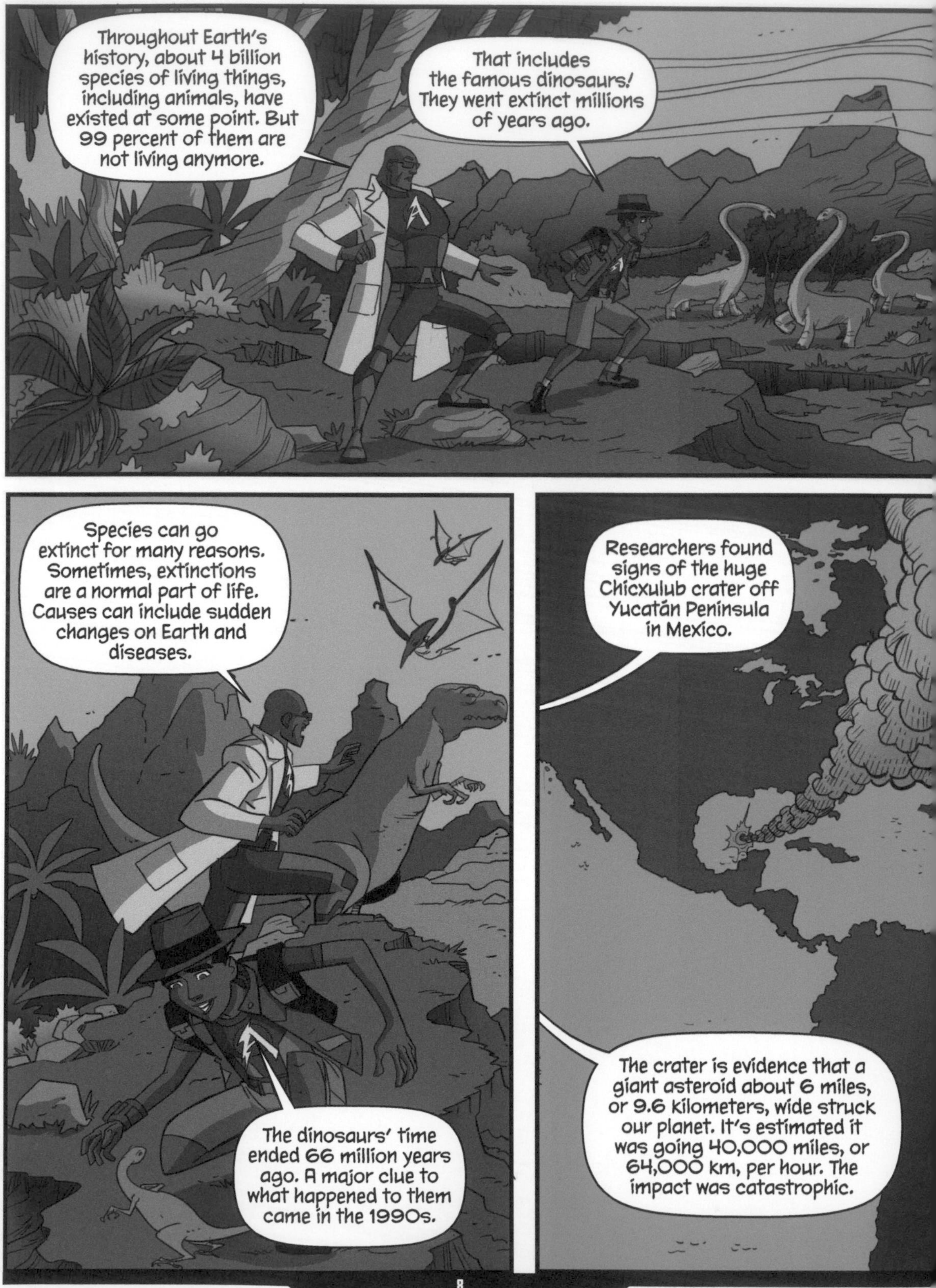
Throughout Earth's history, about 4 billion species of living things, including animals, have existed at some point. But 99 percent of them are not living anymore.
That includes the famous dinosaurs! They went extinct millions of years ago.
Species can go extinct for many reasons. Sometimes, extinctions are a normal part of life. Causes can include sudden changes on Earth and diseases.
The dinosaurs' time ended 66 million years ago. A major clue to what happened to them came in the 1990s.
Researchers found signs of the huge Chicxulub crater off Yucatán Peninsula in Mexico.
The crater is evidence that a giant asteroid about 6 miles, or 9.6 kilometers, wide struck our planet. It's estimated it was going 40,000 miles, or 64,000 km, per hour. The impact was catastrophic.

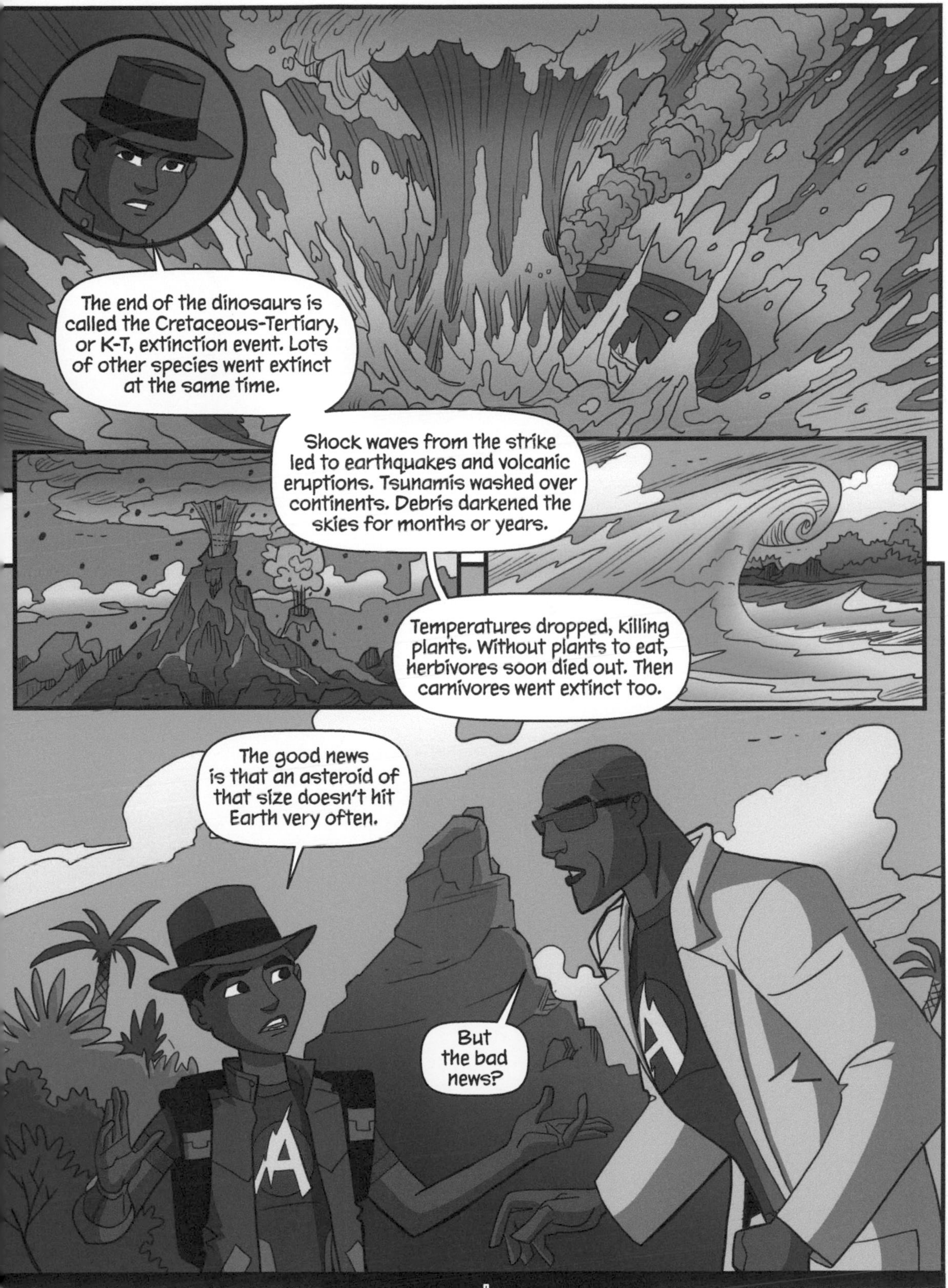
The end of the dinosaurs is called the Cretaceous-Tertiary, or K-T, extinction event. Lots of other species went extinct at the same time.
Shock waves from the strike led to earthquakes and volcanic eruptions. Tsunamis washed over continents. Debris darkened the skies for months or years.
Temperatures dropped, killing plants. Without plants to eat, herbivores soon died out. Then carnivores went extinct too.
The good news is that an asteroid of that size doesn't hit Earth very often.
But the bad news?

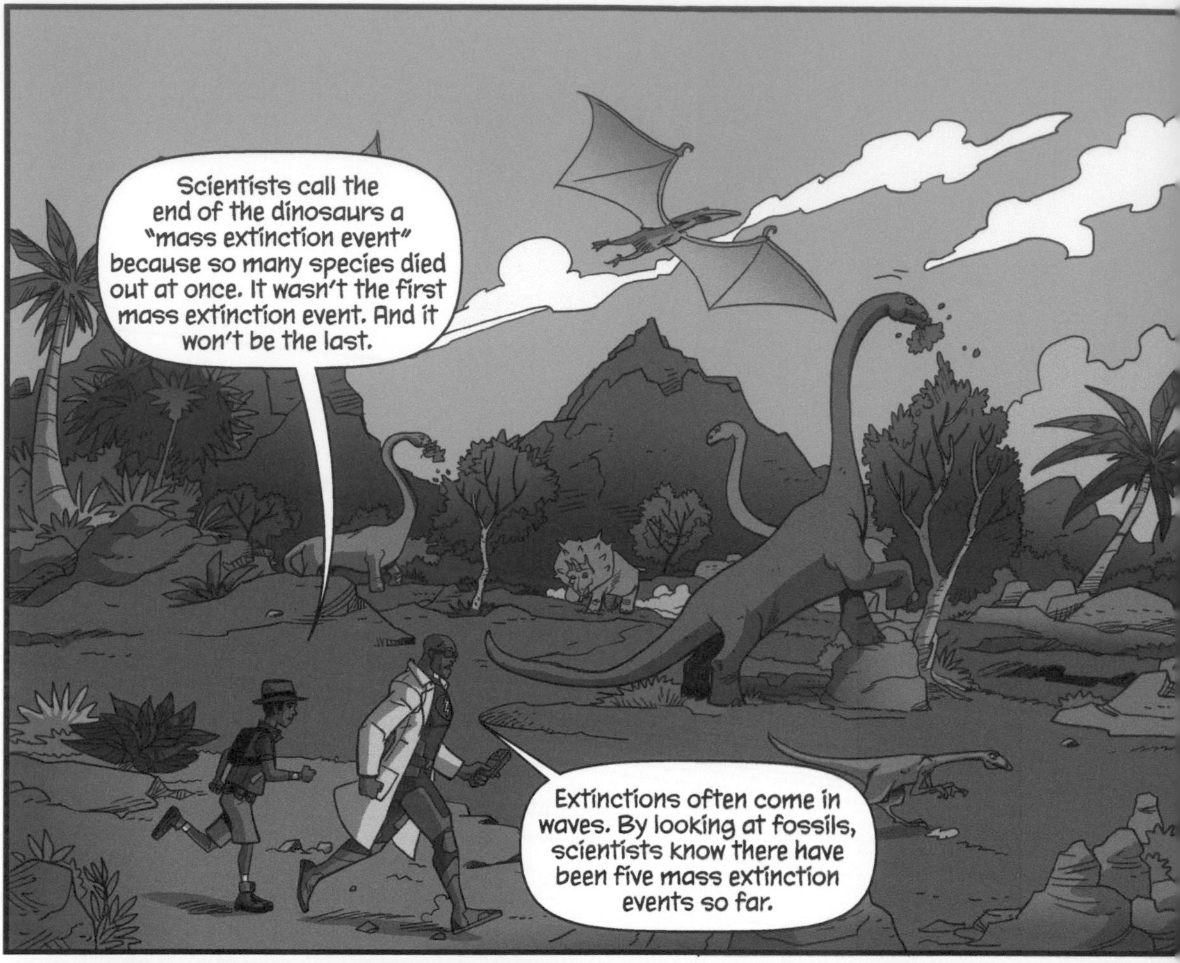
Scientists call the end of the dinosaurs a "mass extinction event" because so many species died out at once. It wasn't the first mass extinction event. And it won't be the last.
Extinctions often come in waves. By looking at fossils, scientists know there have been five mass extinction events so far.

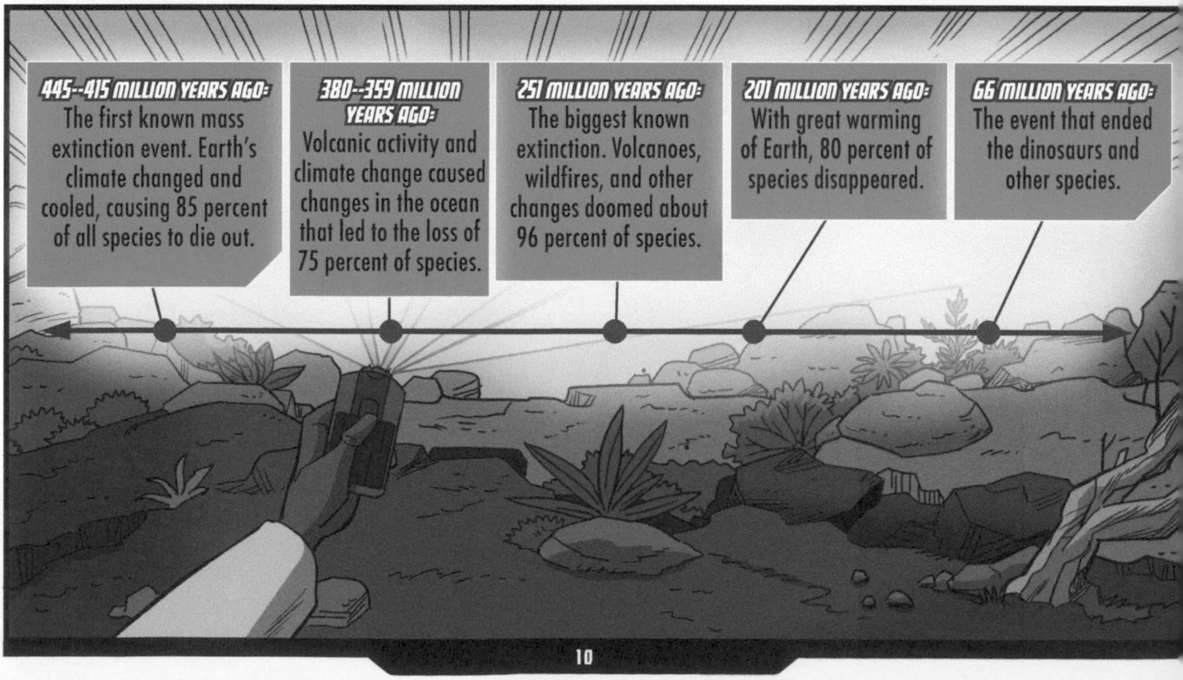
445--415 MILLION YEARS AGO: The first known mass extinction event. Earth's climate changed and cooled, causing 85 percent of all species to die out.
380--359 MILLION YEARS AGO: Volcanic activity and climate change caused changes in the ocean that led to the loss of 75 percent of species.
251 MILLION YEARS AGO: The biggest known extinction. Volcanoes, wildfires, and other changes doomed about 96 percent of species.
201 MILLION YEARS AGO: With great warming of Earth, 80 percent of species disappeared.
66 MILLION YEARS AGO: The event that ended the dinosaurs and other species.

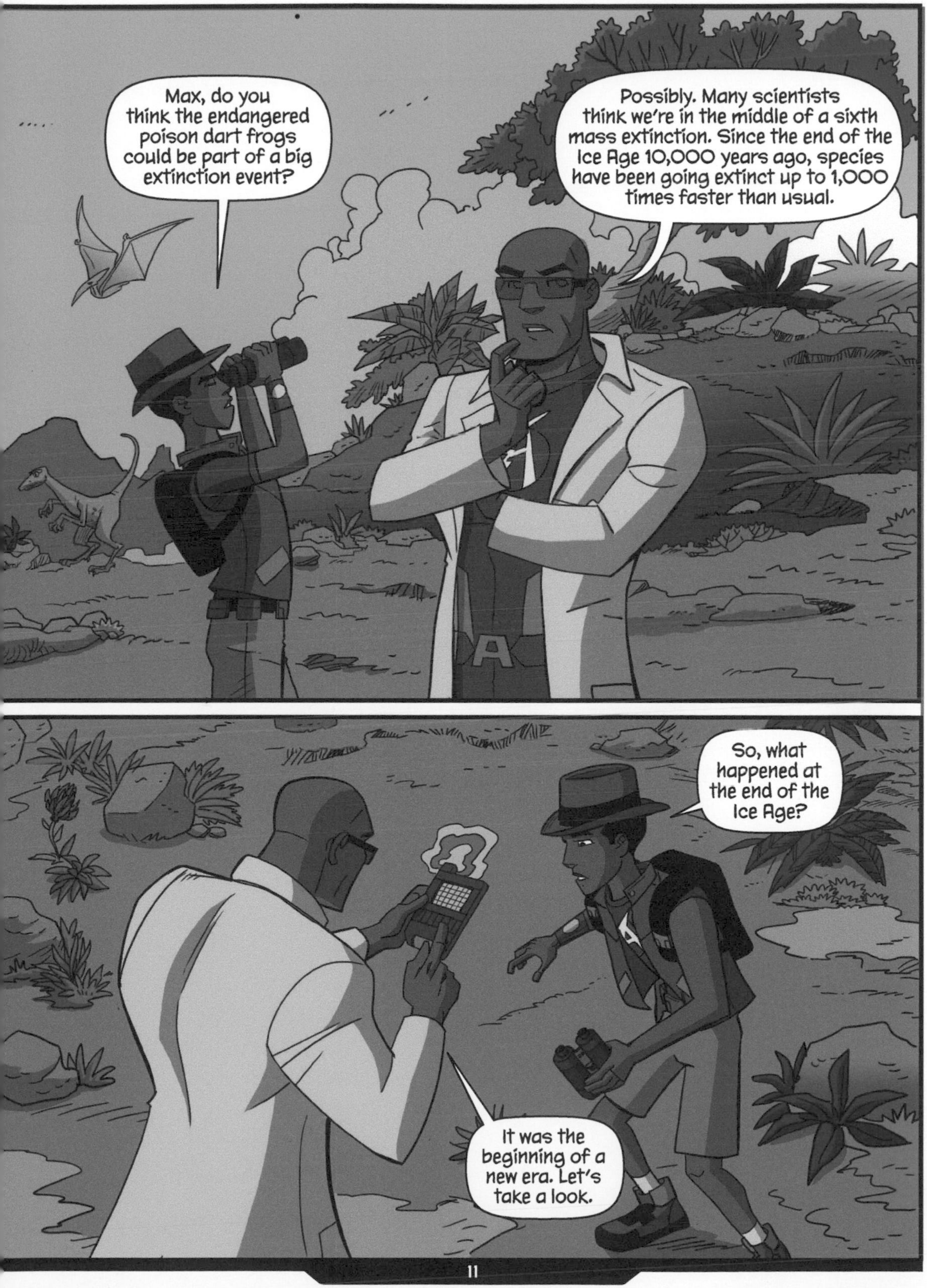

Max, do you think the endangered poison dart frogs could be part of a big extinction event?
Possibly. Many scientists think we're in the middle of a sixth mass extinction. Since the end of the Ice Age 10,000 years ago, species have been going extinct up to 1,000 times faster than usual.
So, what happened at the end of the Ice Age?
It was the beginning of a new era. Let's take a look.

SECTION 2: *THE HUMAN FACTOR*

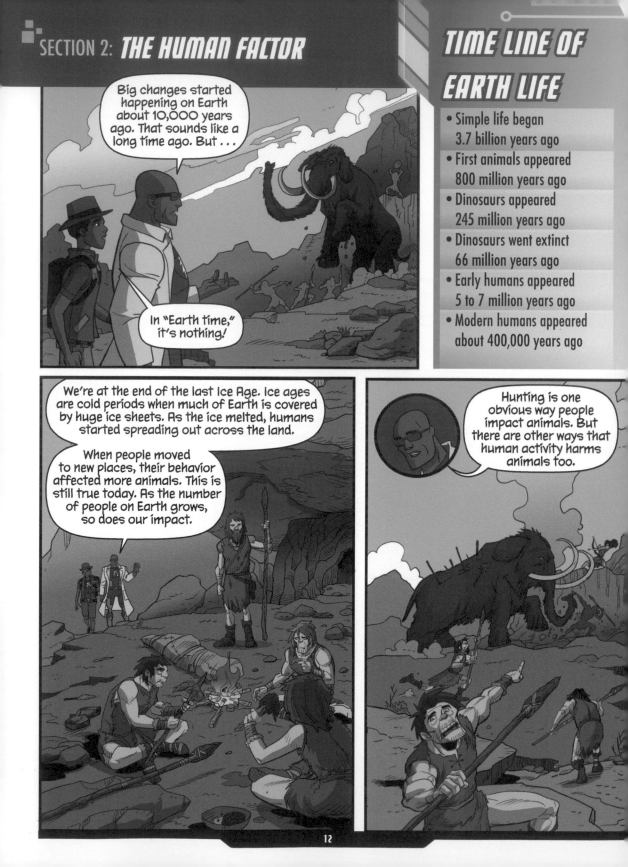

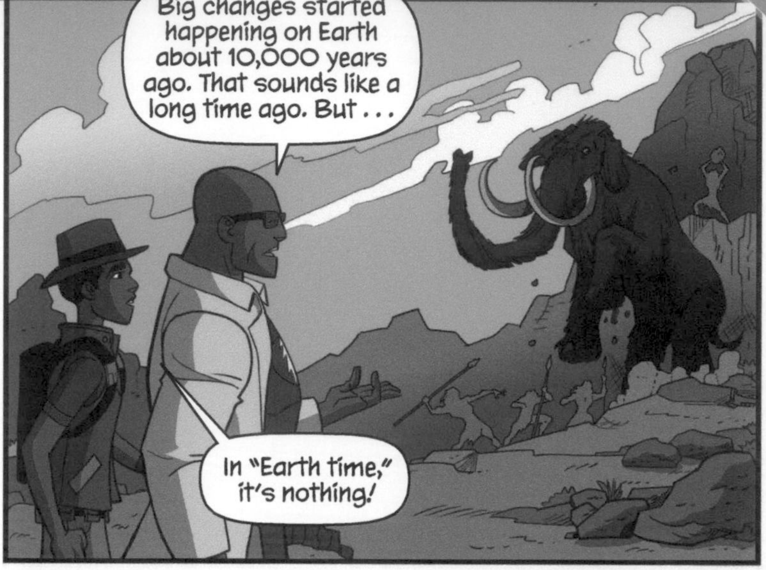
Big changes started happening on Earth about 10,000 years ago. That sounds like a long time ago. But . . .
In "Earth time," it's nothing!

TIME LINE OF EARTH LIFE

- Simple life began 3.7 billion years ago
- First animals appeared 800 million years ago
- Dinosaurs appeared 245 million years ago
- Dinosaurs went extinct 66 million years ago
- Early humans appeared 5 to 7 million years ago
- Modern humans appeared about 400,000 years ago

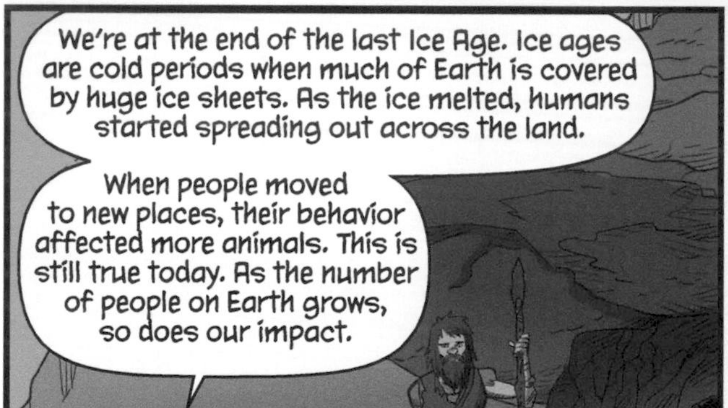
We're at the end of the last Ice Age. Ice ages are cold periods when much of Earth is covered by huge ice sheets. As the ice melted, humans started spreading out across the land.
When people moved to new places, their behavior affected more animals. This is still true today. As the number of people on Earth grows, so does our impact.

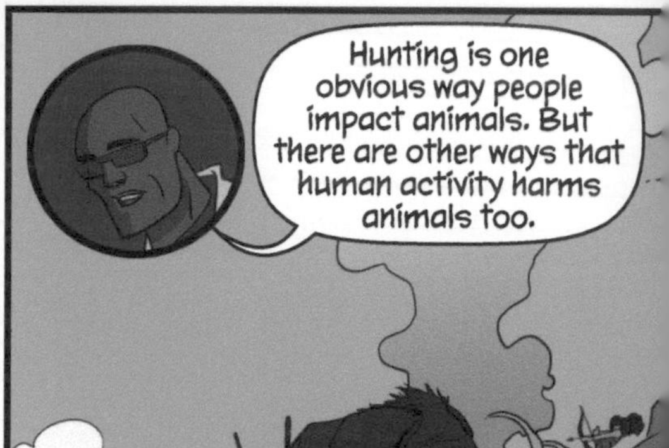
Hunting is one obvious way people impact animals. But there are other ways that human activity harms animals too.

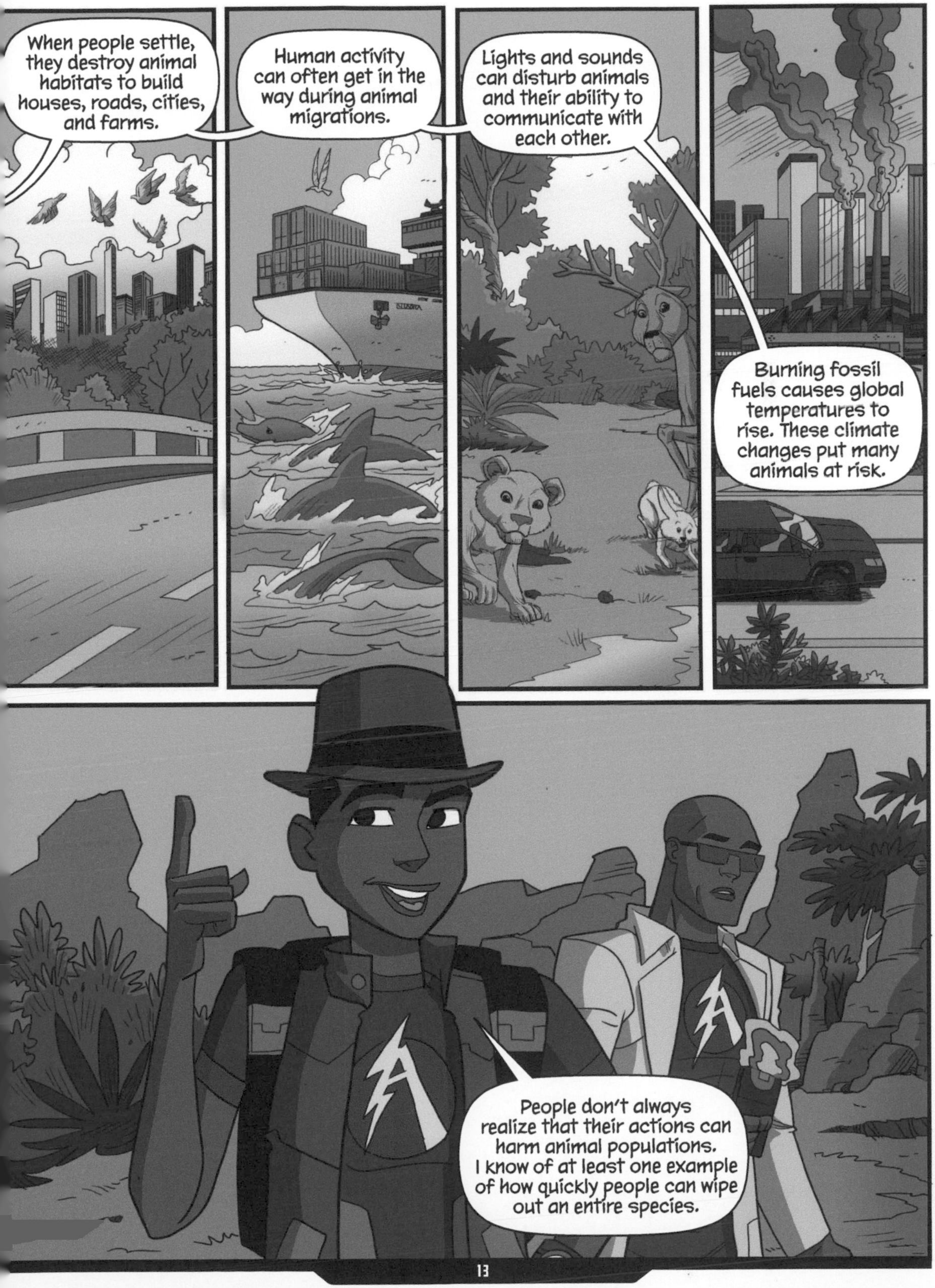
When people settle, they destroy animal habitats to build houses, roads, cities, and farms.
Human activity can often get in the way during animal migrations.
Lights and sounds can disturb animals and their ability to communicate with each other.
Burning fossil fuels causes global temperatures to rise. These climate changes put many animals at risk.
People don't always realize that their actions can harm animal populations. I know of at least one example of how quickly people can wipe out an entire species.

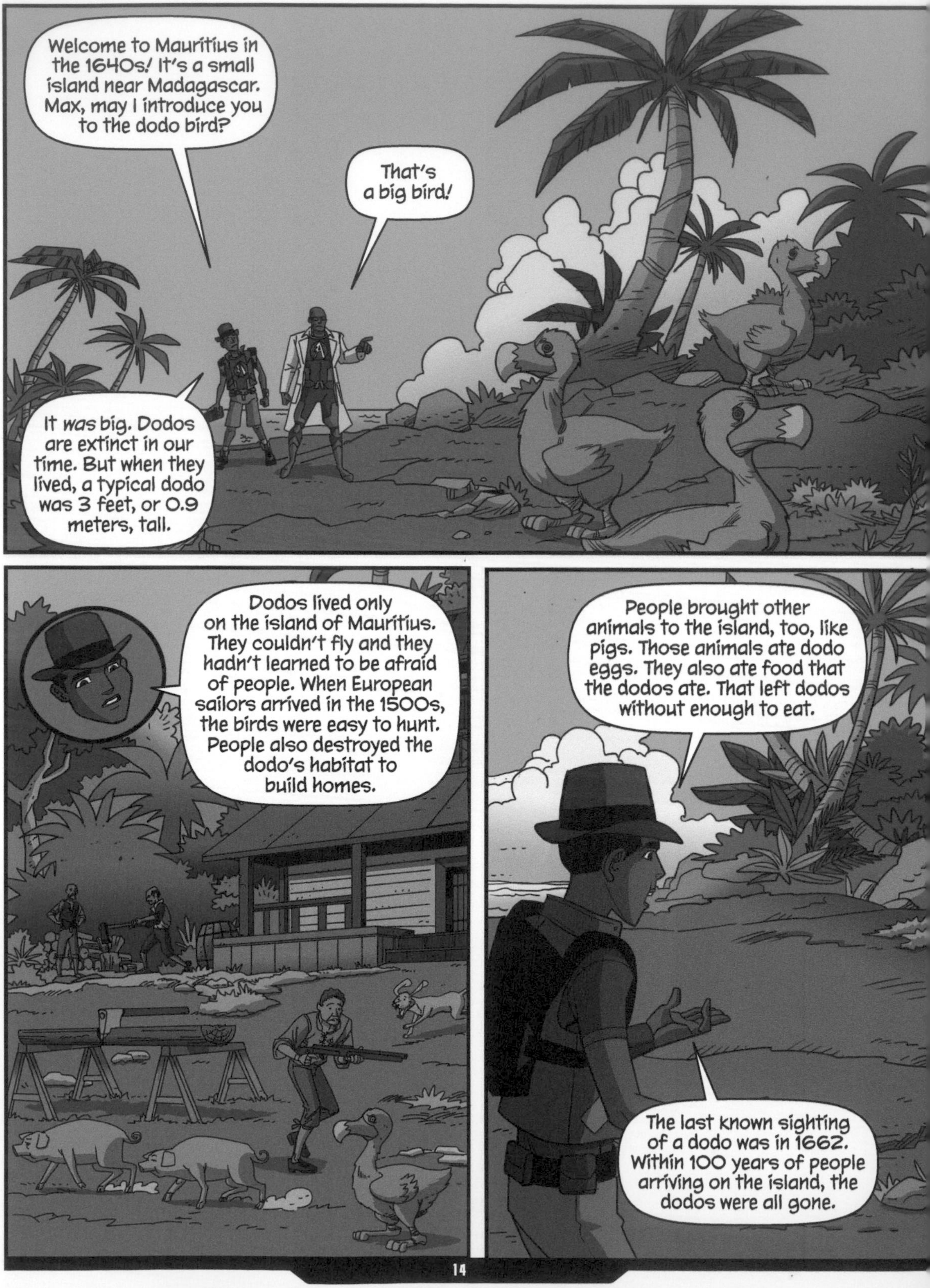

Welcome to Mauritius in the 1640s! It's a small island near Madagascar. Max, may I introduce you to the dodo bird?
That's a big bird!
It *was* big. Dodos are extinct in our time. But when they lived, a typical dodo was 3 feet, or 0.9 meters, tall.
Dodos lived only on the island of Mauritius. They couldn't fly and they hadn't learned to be afraid of people. When European sailors arrived in the 1500s, the birds were easy to hunt. People also destroyed the dodo's habitat to build homes.
People brought other animals to the island, too, like pigs. Those animals ate dodo eggs. They also ate food that the dodos ate. That left dodos without enough to eat.
The last known sighting of a dodo was in 1662. Within 100 years of people arriving on the island, the dodos were all gone.

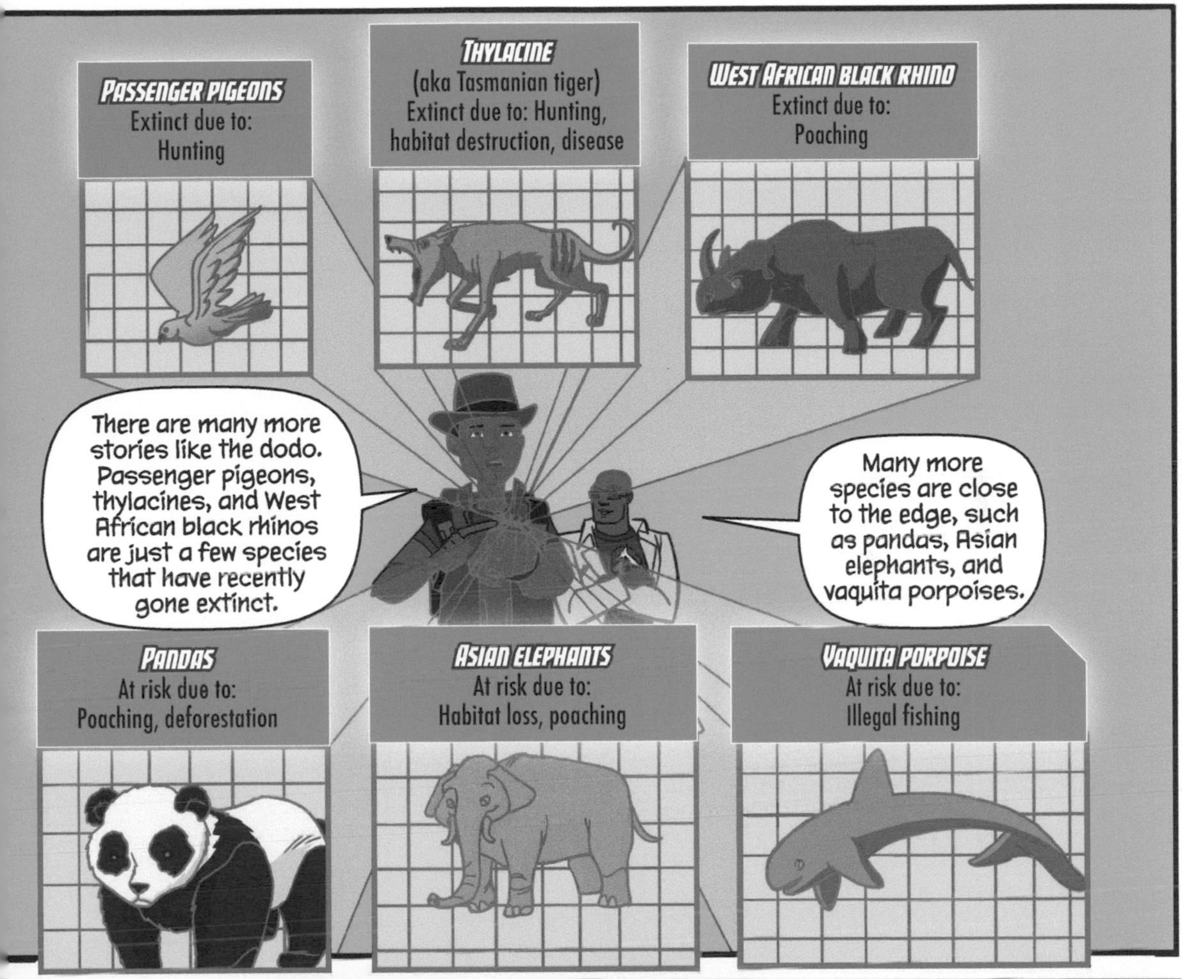
PASSENGER PIGEONS
Extinct due to:
Hunting
THYLACINE
(aka Tasmanian tiger)
Extinct due to: Hunting,
habitat destruction, disease
WEST AFRICAN BLACK RHINO
Extinct due to:
Poaching
There are many more stories like the dodo. Passenger pigeons, thylacines, and West African black rhinos are just a few species that have recently gone extinct.
Many more species are close to the edge, such as pandas, Asian elephants, and vaquita porpoises.
PANDAS
At risk due to:
Poaching, deforestation
ASIAN ELEPHANTS
At risk due to:
Habitat loss, poaching
VAQUITA PORPOISE
At risk due to:
Illegal fishing

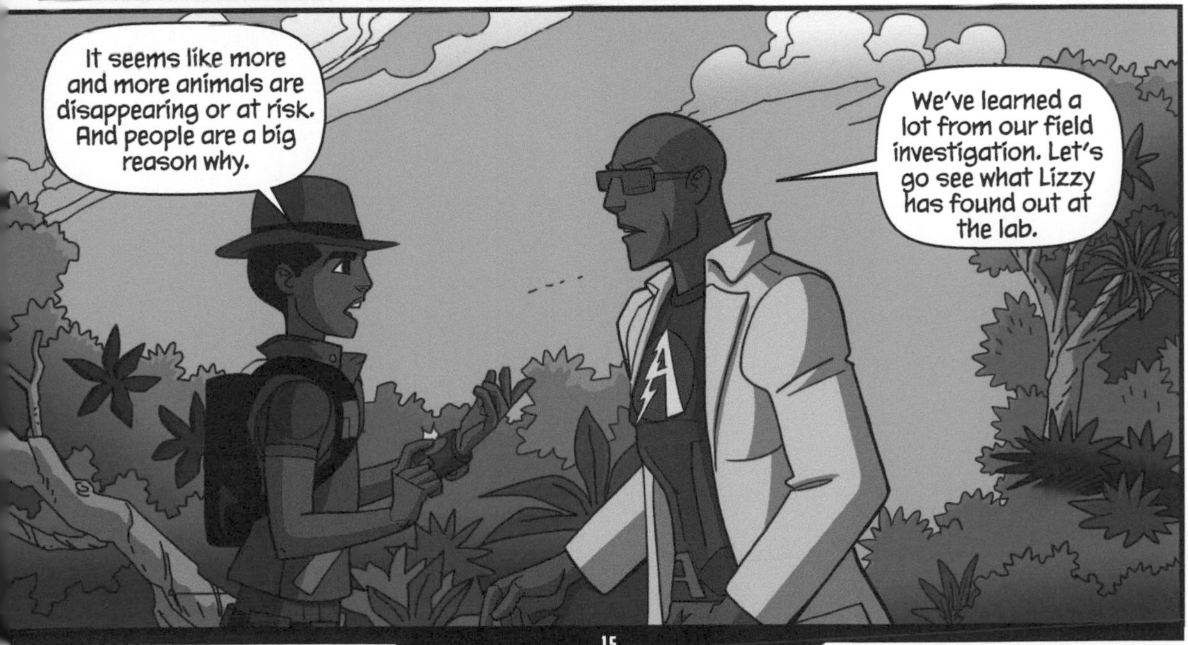
It seems like more and more animals are disappearing or at risk. And people are a big reason why.
We've learned a lot from our field investigation. Let's go see what Lizzy has found out at the lab.

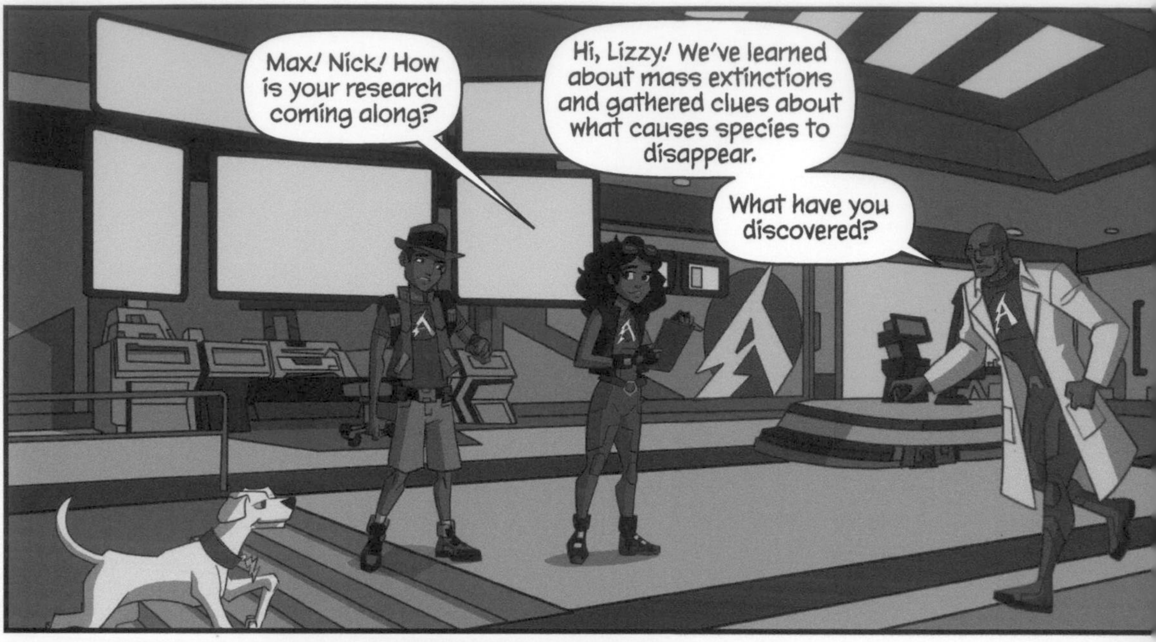
Max! Nick! How is your research coming along?
Hi, Lizzy! We've learned about mass extinctions and gathered clues about what causes species to disappear.
What have you discovered?

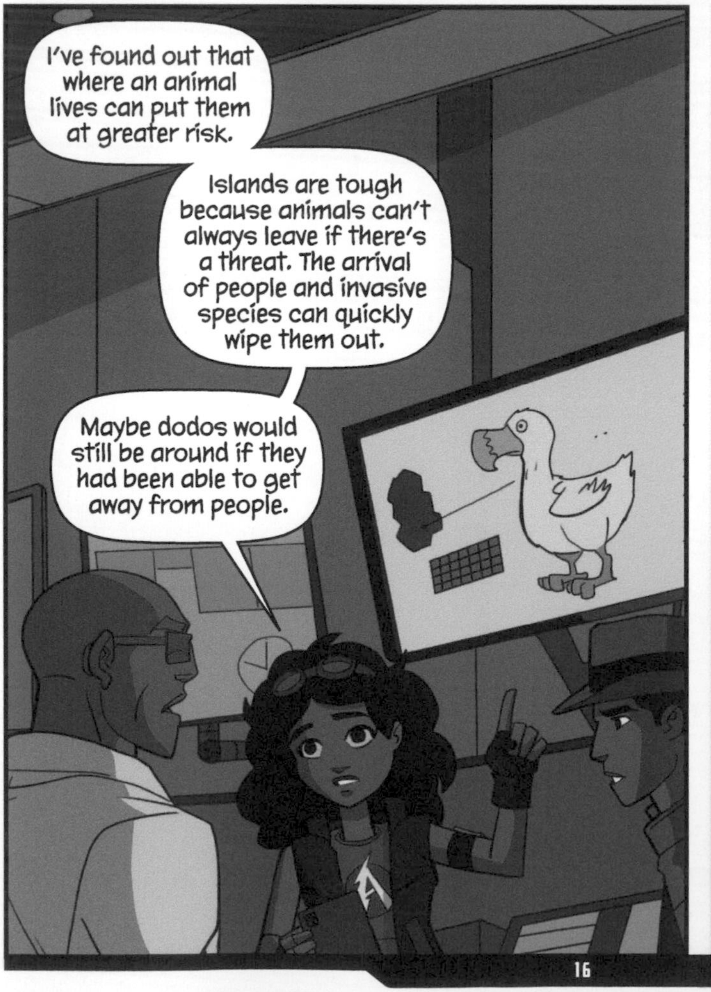
I've found out that where an animal lives can put them at greater risk.
Islands are tough because animals can't always leave if there's a threat. The arrival of people and invasive species can quickly wipe them out.
Maybe dodos would still be around if they had been able to get away from people.

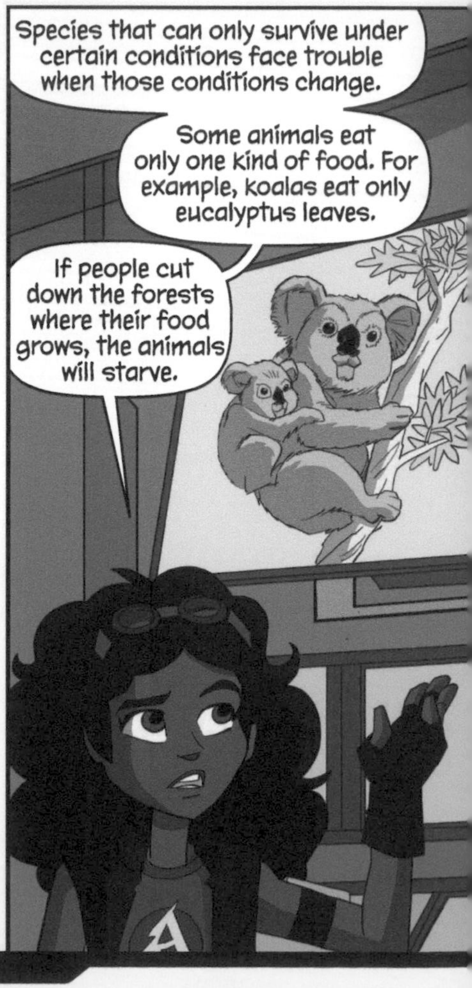
Species that can only survive under certain conditions face trouble when those conditions change.
Some animals eat only one kind of food. For example, koalas eat only eucalyptus leaves.
If people cut down the forests where their food grows, the animals will starve.

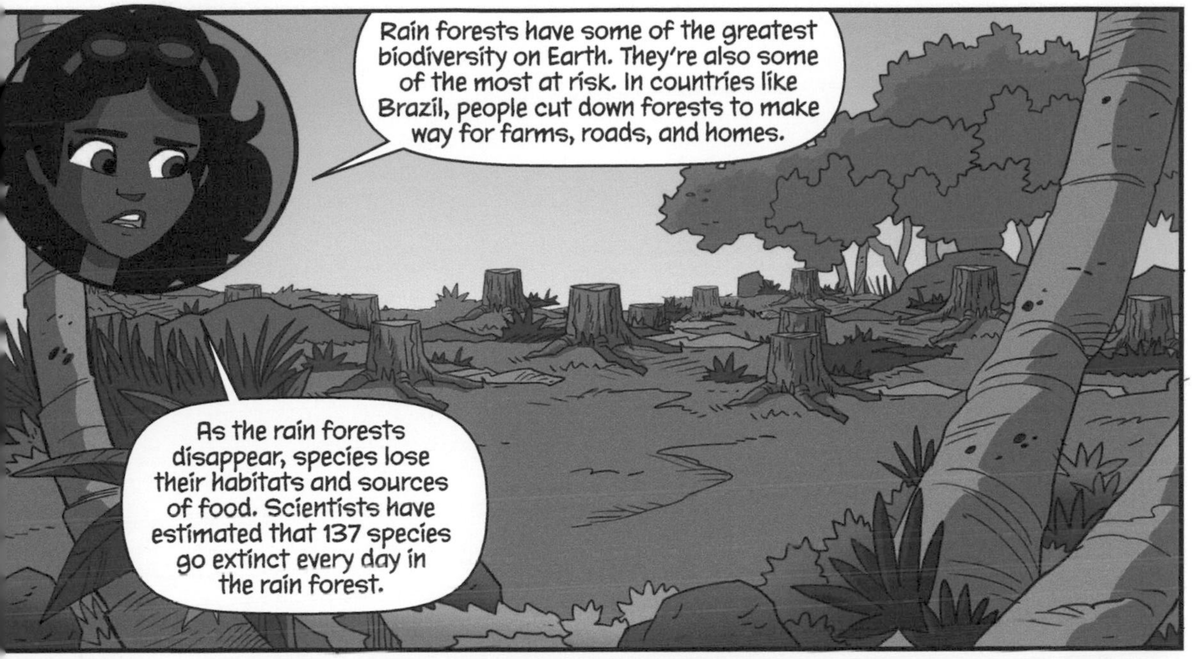
Rain forests have some of the greatest biodiversity on Earth. They're also some of the most at risk. In countries like Brazil, people cut down forests to make way for farms, roads, and homes.
As the rain forests disappear, species lose their habitats and sources of food. Scientists have estimated that 137 species go extinct every day in the rain forest.

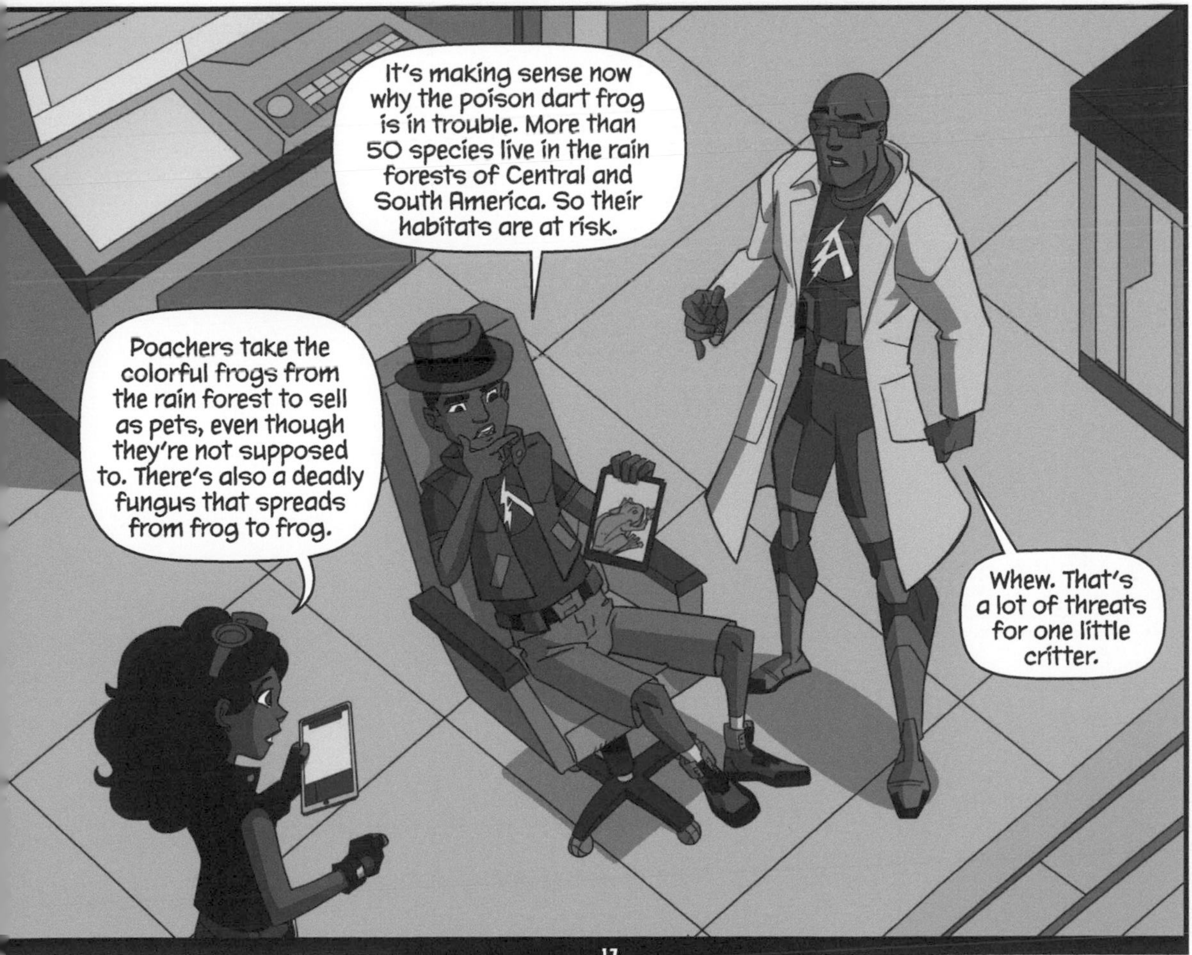
It's making sense now why the poison dart frog is in trouble. More than 50 species live in the rain forests of Central and South America. So their habitats are at risk.
Poachers take the colorful frogs from the rain forest to sell as pets, even though they're not supposed to. There's also a deadly fungus that spreads from frog to frog.
Whew. That's a lot of threats for one little critter.

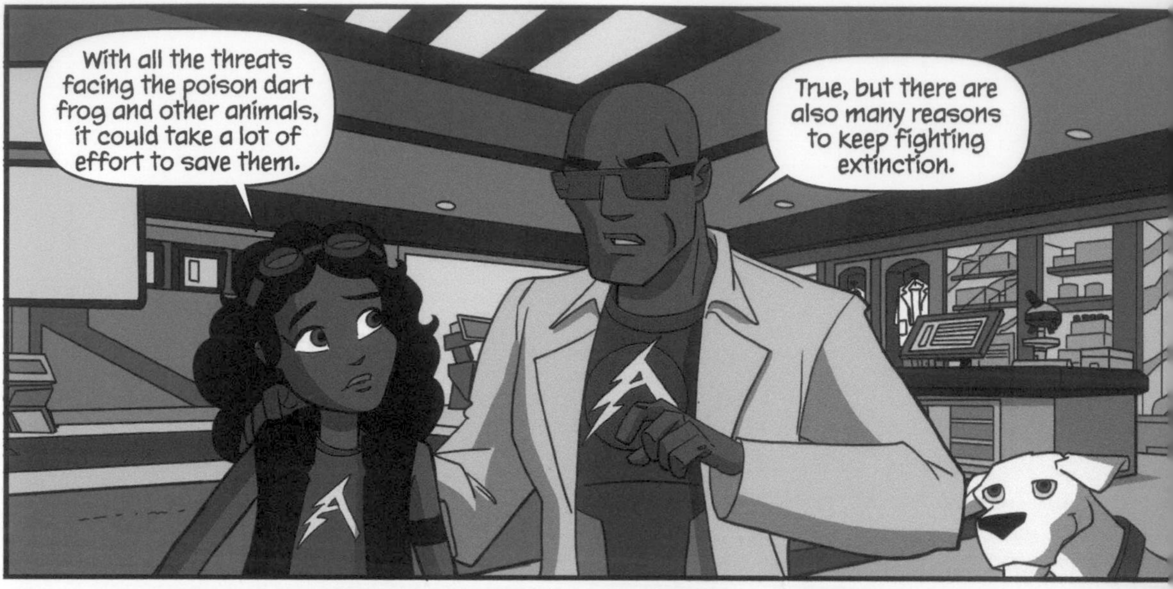

With all the threats facing the poison dart frog and other animals, it could take a lot of effort to save them.
True, but there are also many reasons to keep fighting extinction.

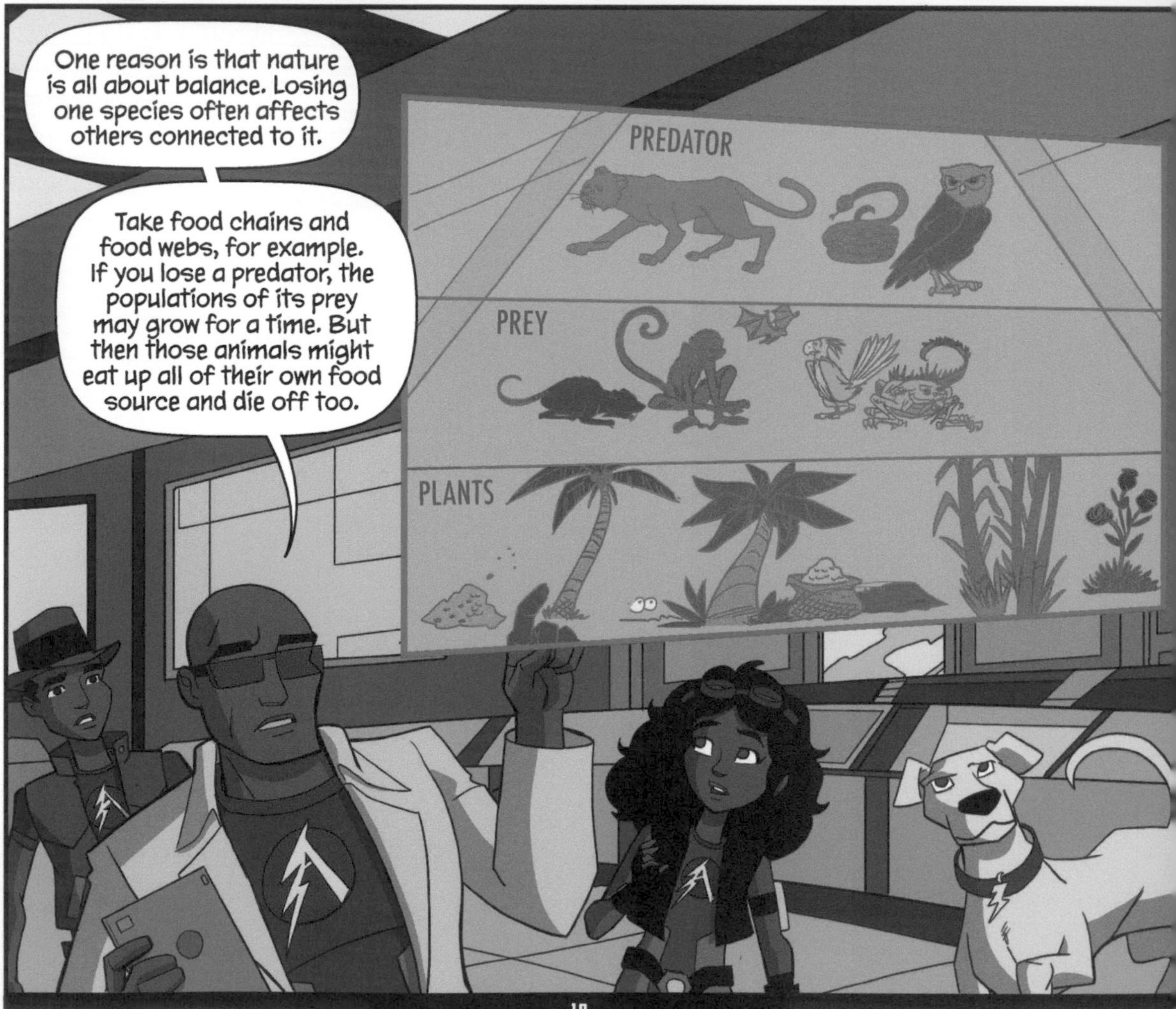

One reason is that nature is all about balance. Losing one species often affects others connected to it.
Take food chains and food webs, for example. If you lose a predator, the populations of its prey may grow for a time. But then those animals might eat up all of their own food source and die off too.
PREDATOR
PREY
PLANTS

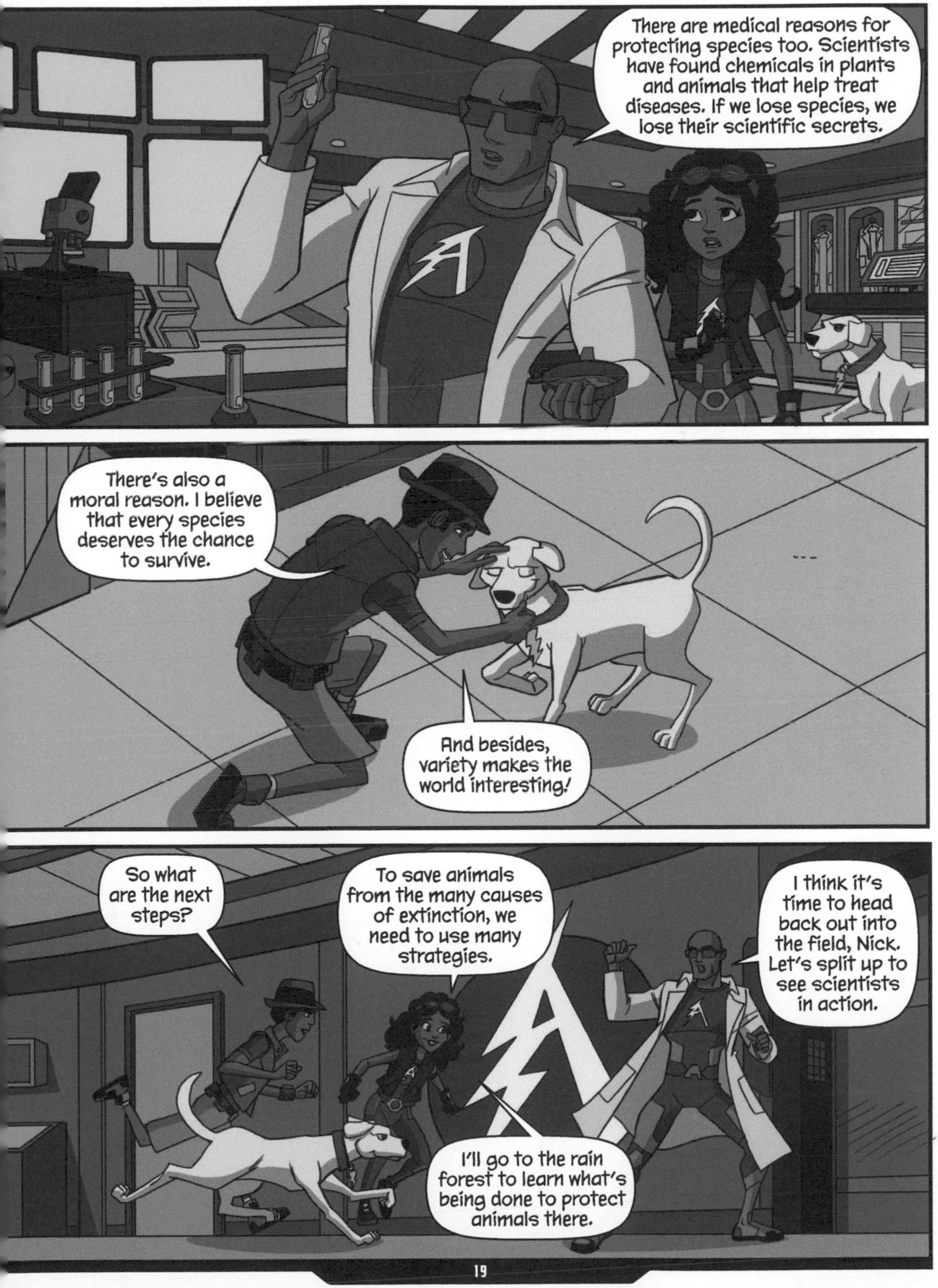
There are medical reasons for protecting species too. Scientists have found chemicals in plants and animals that help treat diseases. If we lose species, we lose their scientific secrets.
There's also a moral reason. I believe that every species deserves the chance to survive.
...
And besides, variety makes the world interesting!
So what are the next steps?
To save animals from the many causes of extinction, we need to use many strategies.
I think it's time to head back out into the field, Nick. Let's split up to see scientists in action.
I'll go to the rain forest to learn what's being done to protect animals there.

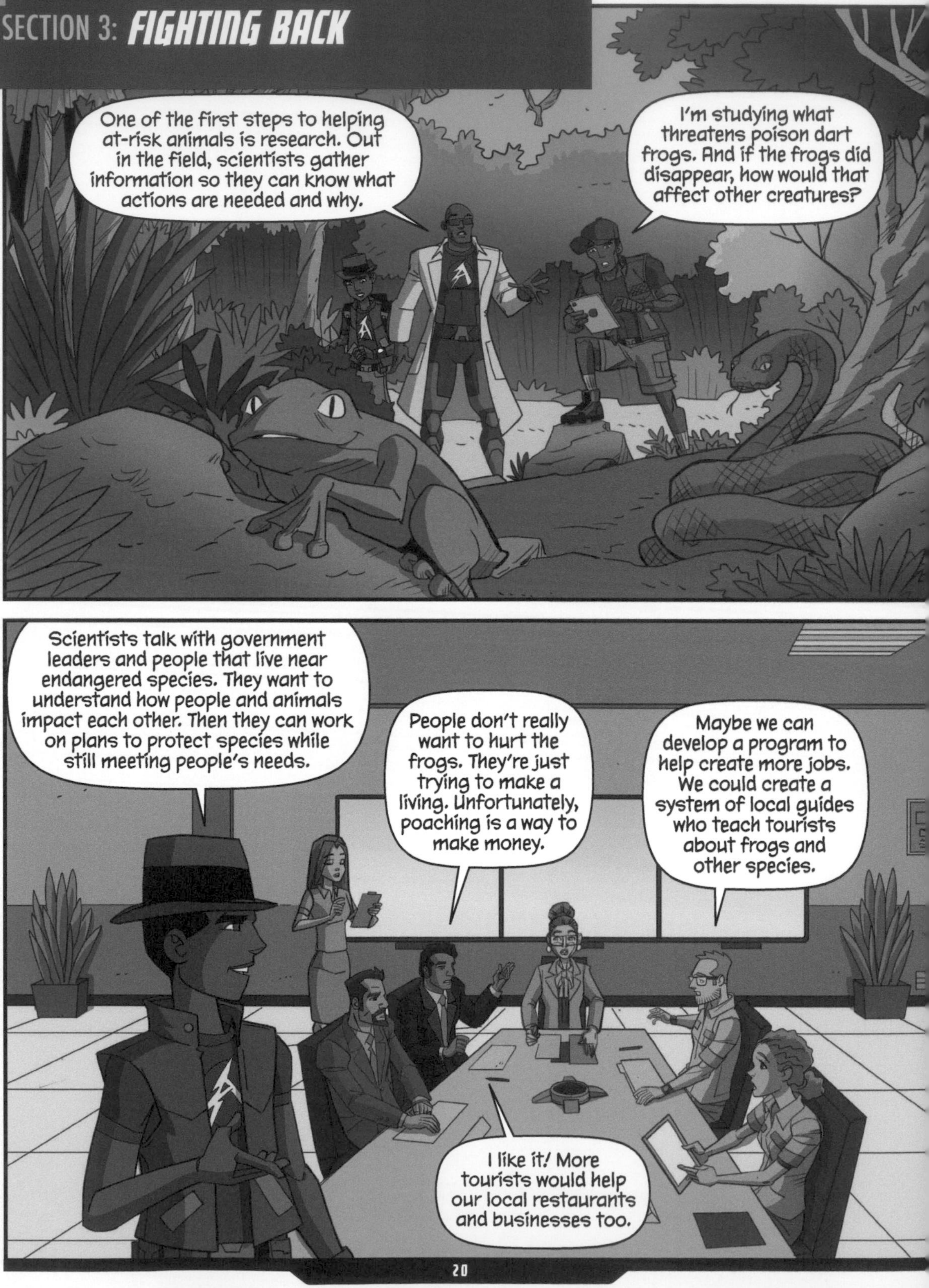
One of the first steps to helping at-risk animals is research. Out in the field, scientists gather information so they can know what actions are needed and why.
I'm studying what threatens poison dart frogs. And if the frogs did disappear, how would that affect other creatures?
Scientists talk with government leaders and people that live near endangered species. They want to understand how people and animals impact each other. Then they can work on plans to protect species while still meeting people's needs.
People don't really want to hurt the frogs. They're just trying to make a living. Unfortunately, poaching is a way to make money.
Maybe we can develop a program to help create more jobs. We could create a system of local guides who teach tourists about frogs and other species.
I like it! More tourists would help our local restaurants and businesses too.

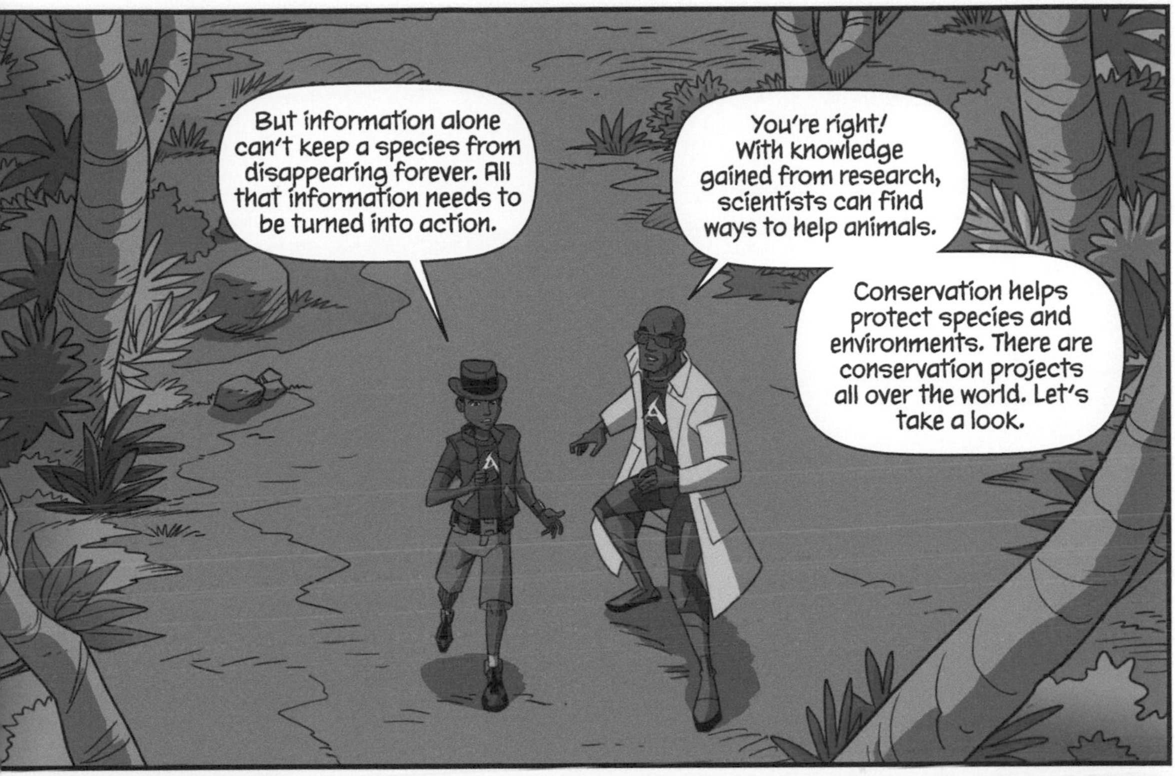
But information alone can't keep a species from disappearing forever. All that information needs to be turned into action.
You're right! With knowledge gained from research, scientists can find ways to help animals.
Conservation helps protect species and environments. There are conservation projects all over the world. Let's take a look.

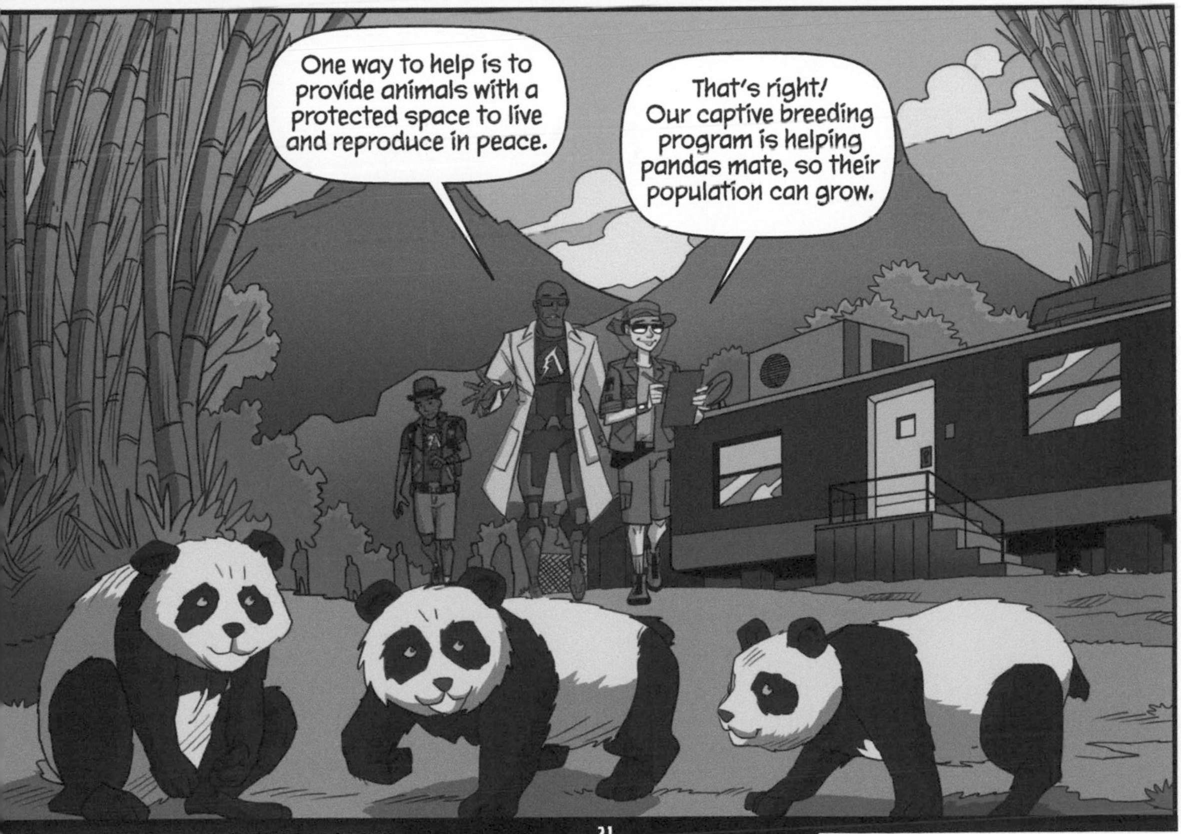
One way to help is to provide animals with a protected space to live and reproduce in peace.
That's right! Our captive breeding program is helping pandas mate, so their population can grow.

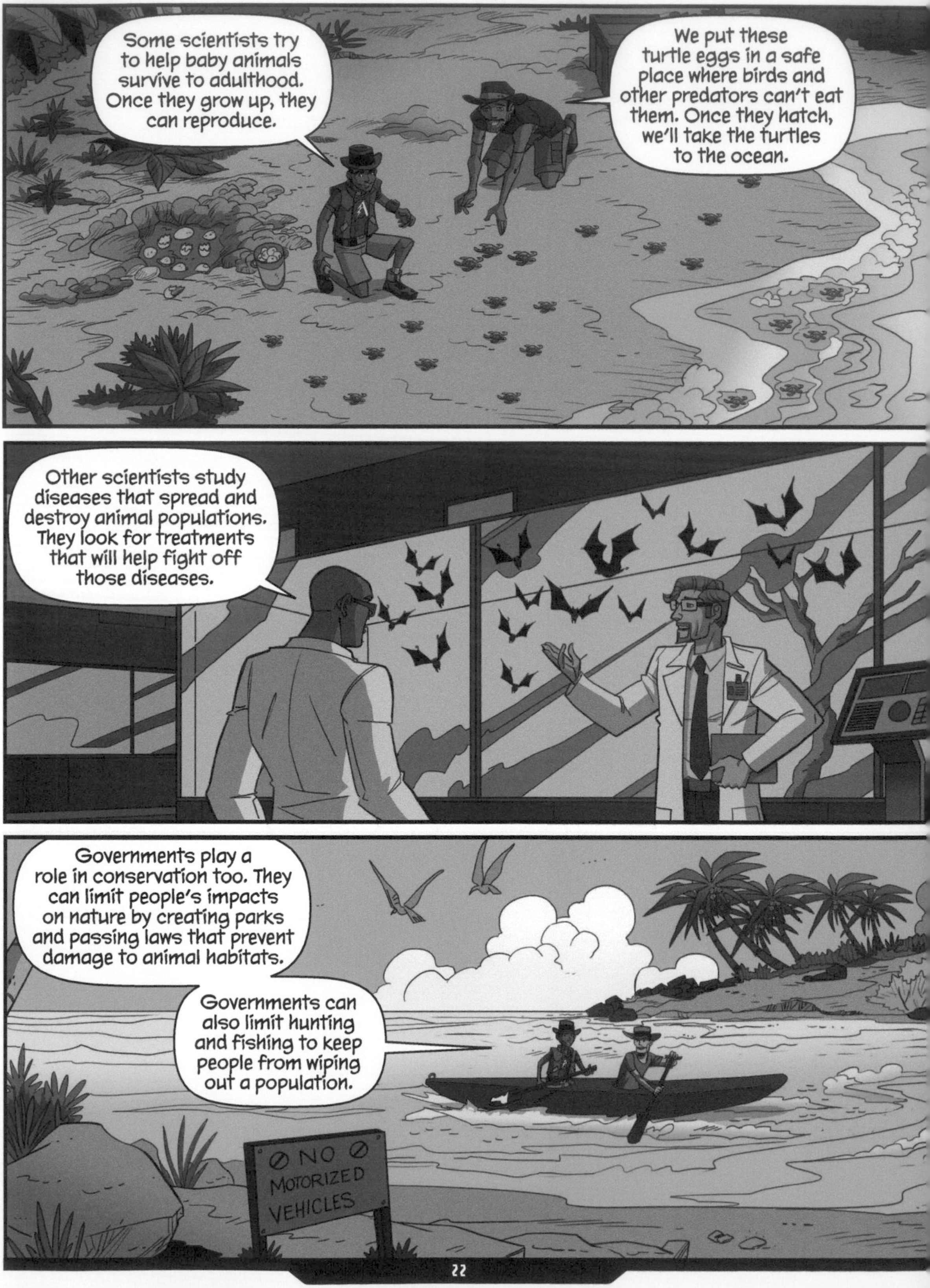
Some scientists try to help baby animals survive to adulthood. Once they grow up, they can reproduce.
We put these turtle eggs in a safe place where birds and other predators can't eat them. Once they hatch, we'll take the turtles to the ocean.
Other scientists study diseases that spread and destroy animal populations. They look for treatments that will help fight off those diseases.
Governments play a role in conservation too. They can limit people's impacts on nature by creating parks and passing laws that prevent damage to animal habitats.
Governments can also limit hunting and fishing to keep people from wiping out a population.
NO MOTORIZED VEHICLES

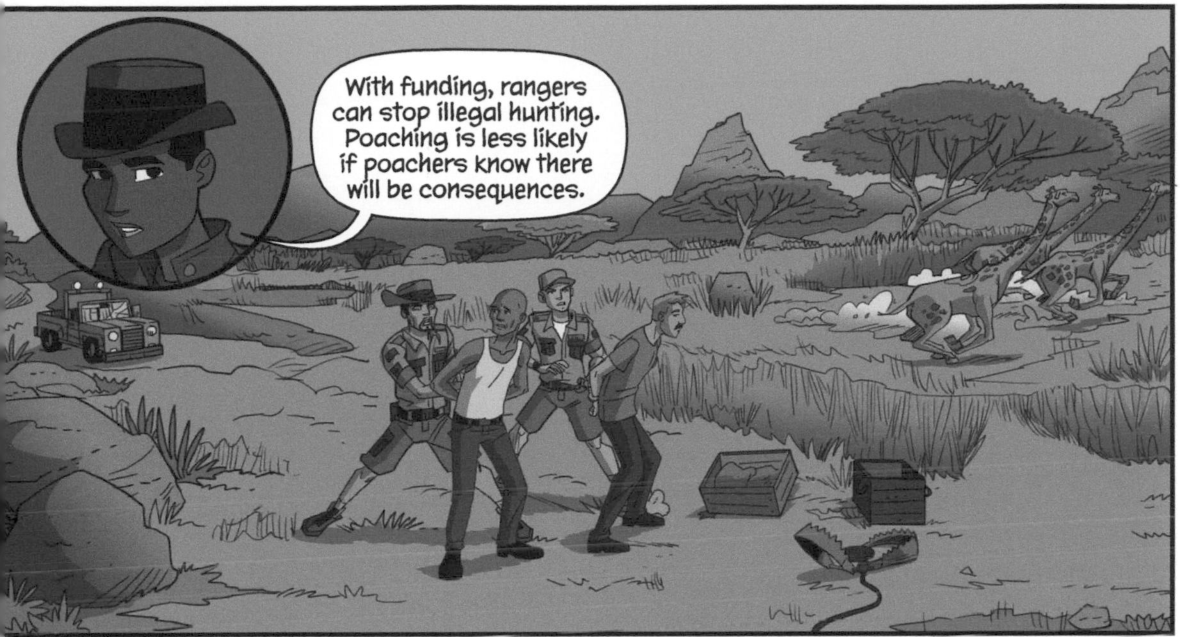
With funding, rangers can stop illegal hunting. Poaching is less likely if poachers know there will be consequences.

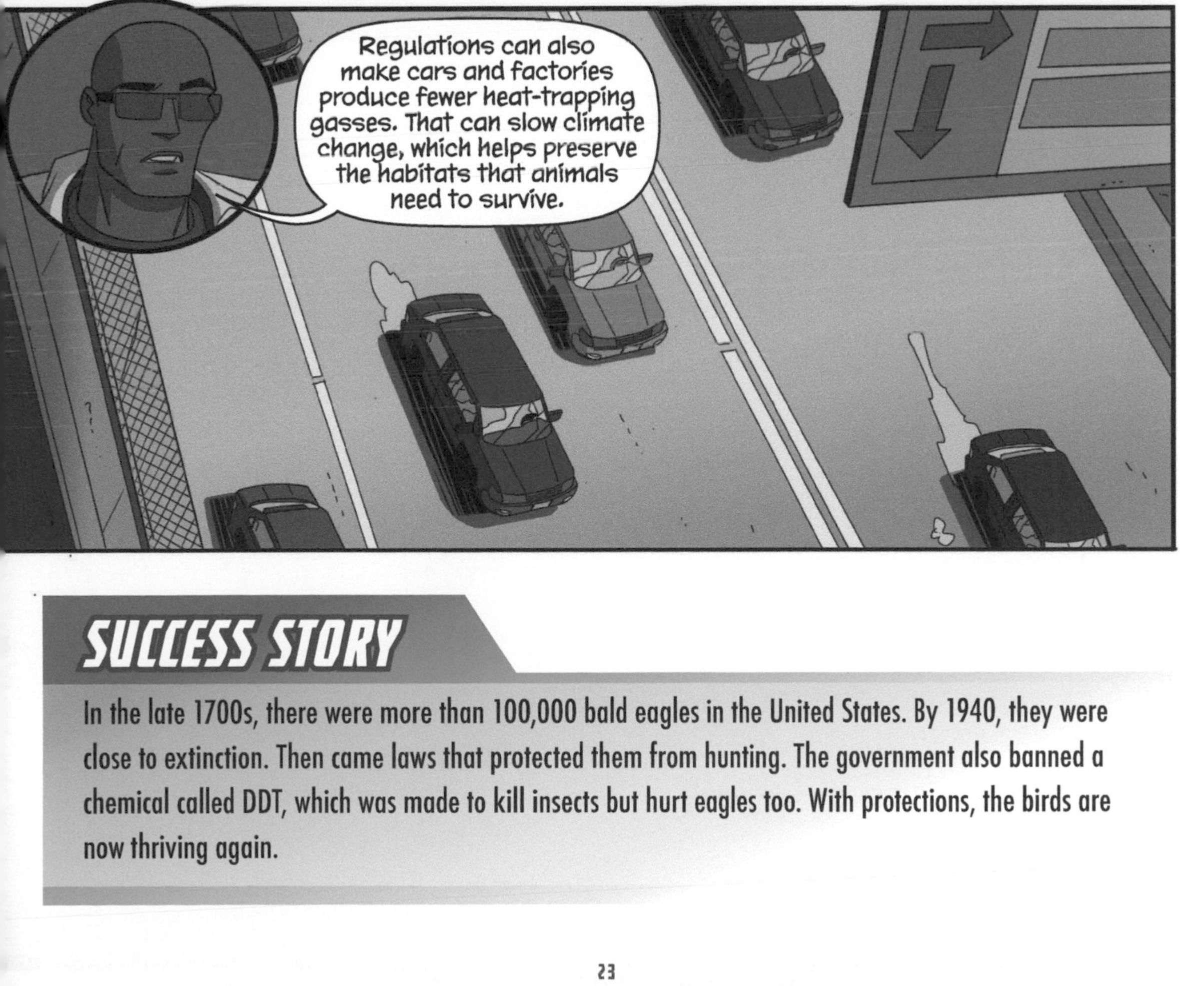
Regulations can also make cars and factories produce fewer heat-trapping gasses. That can slow climate change, which helps preserve the habitats that animals need to survive.

SUCCESS STORY

In the late 1700s, there were more than 100,000 bald eagles in the United States. By 1940, they were close to extinction. Then came laws that protected them from hunting. The government also banned a chemical called DDT, which was made to kill insects but hurt eagles too. With protections, the birds are now thriving again.

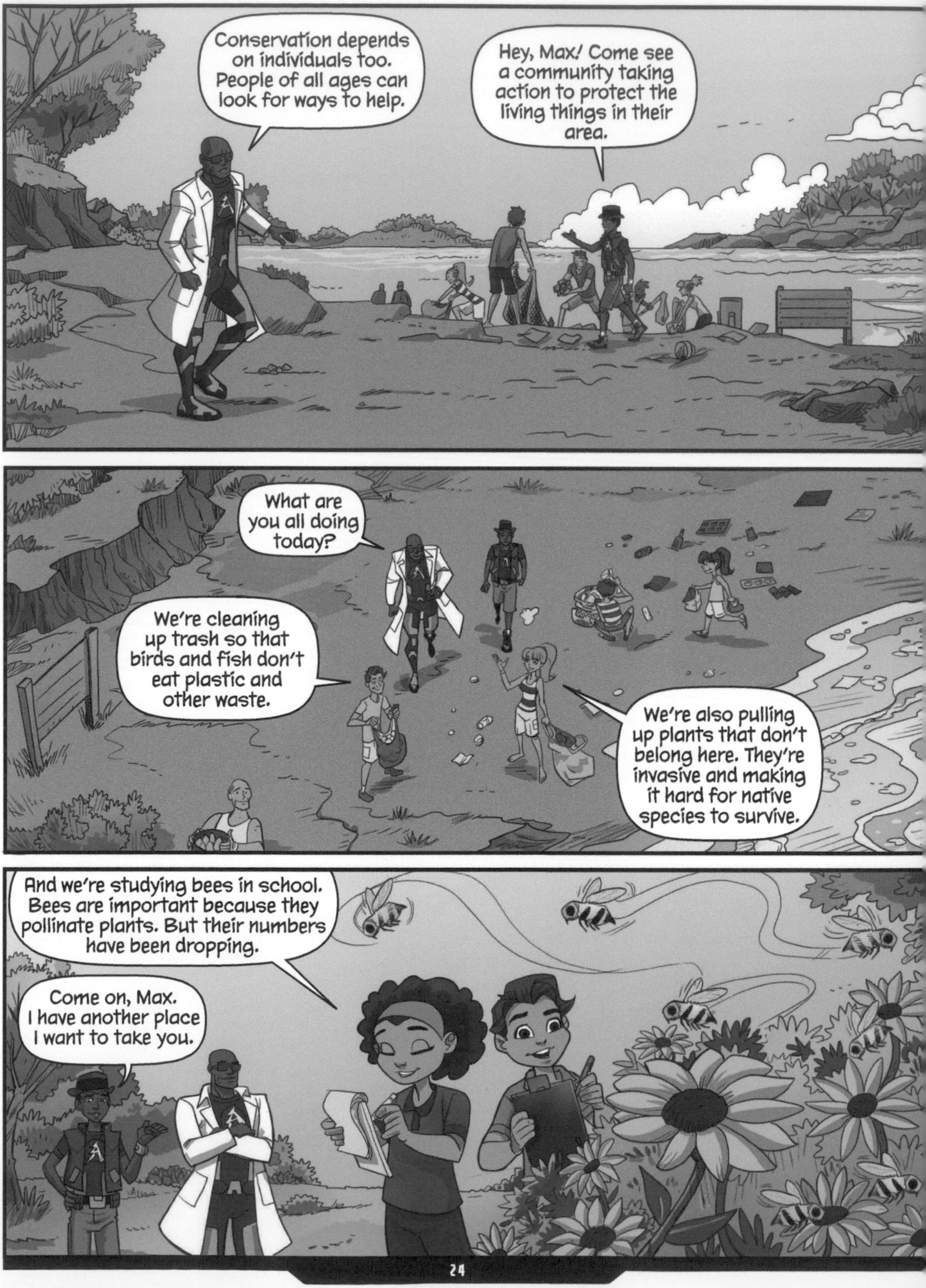
Conservation depends on individuals too. People of all ages can look for ways to help.
Hey, Max! Come see a community taking action to protect the living things in their area.
What are you all doing today?
We're cleaning up trash so that birds and fish don't eat plastic and other waste.
We're also pulling up plants that don't belong here. They're invasive and making it hard for native species to survive.
And we're studying bees in school. Bees are important because they pollinate plants. But their numbers have been dropping.
Come on, Max. I have another place I want to take you.

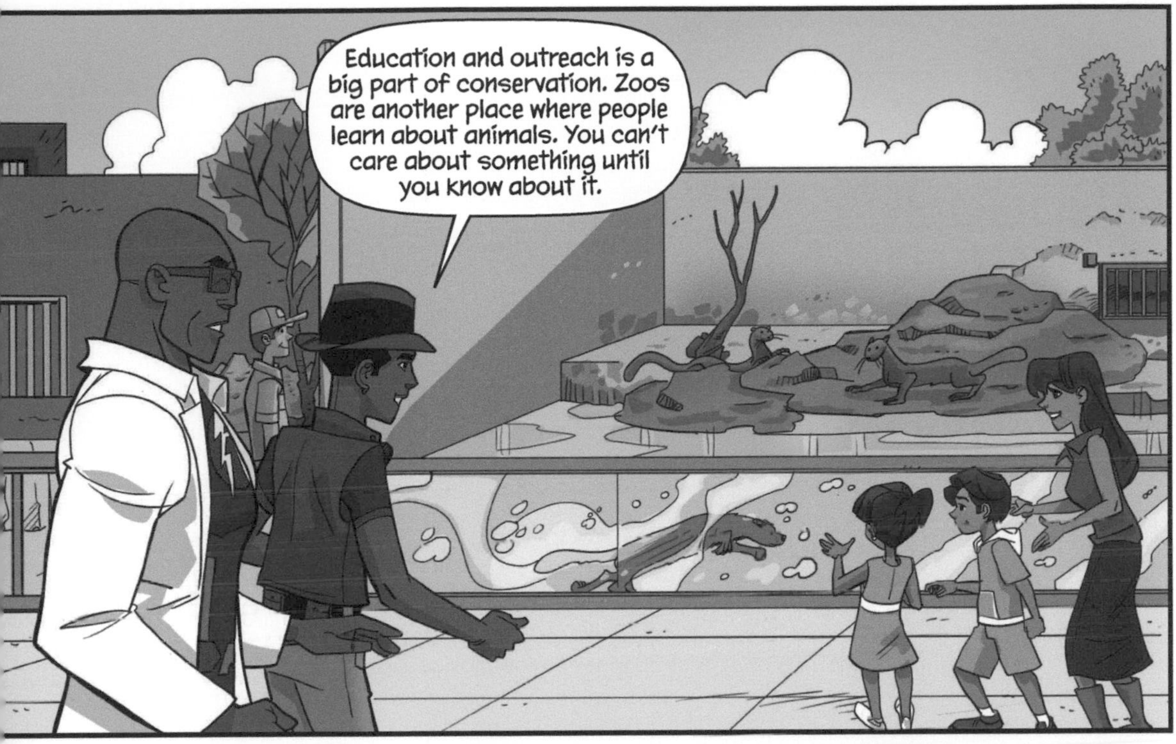
Education and outreach is a big part of conservation. Zoos are another place where people learn about animals. You can't care about something until you know about it.

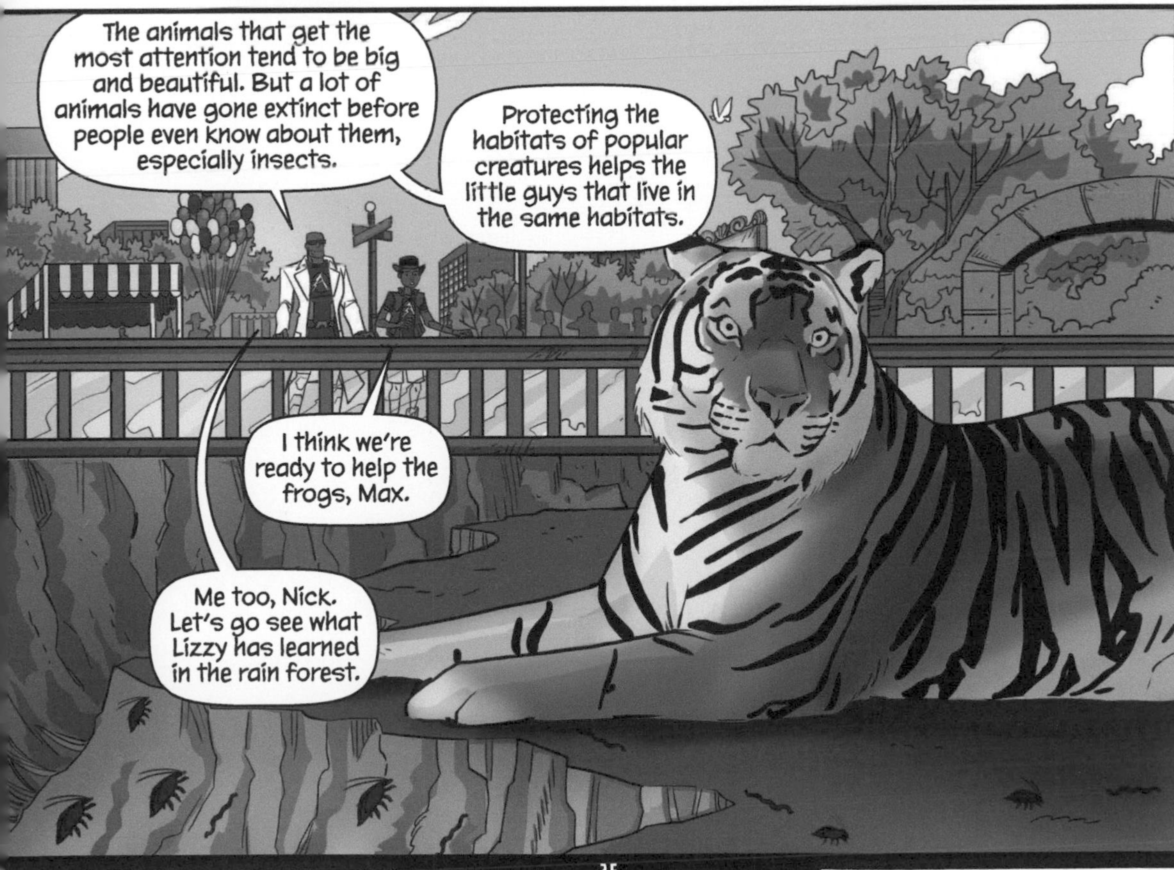
The animals that get the most attention tend to be big and beautiful. But a lot of animals have gone extinct before people even know about them, especially insects.
Protecting the habitats of popular creatures helps the little guys that live in the same habitats.
I think we're ready to help the frogs, Max.
Me too, Nick. Let's go see what Lizzy has learned in the rain forest.

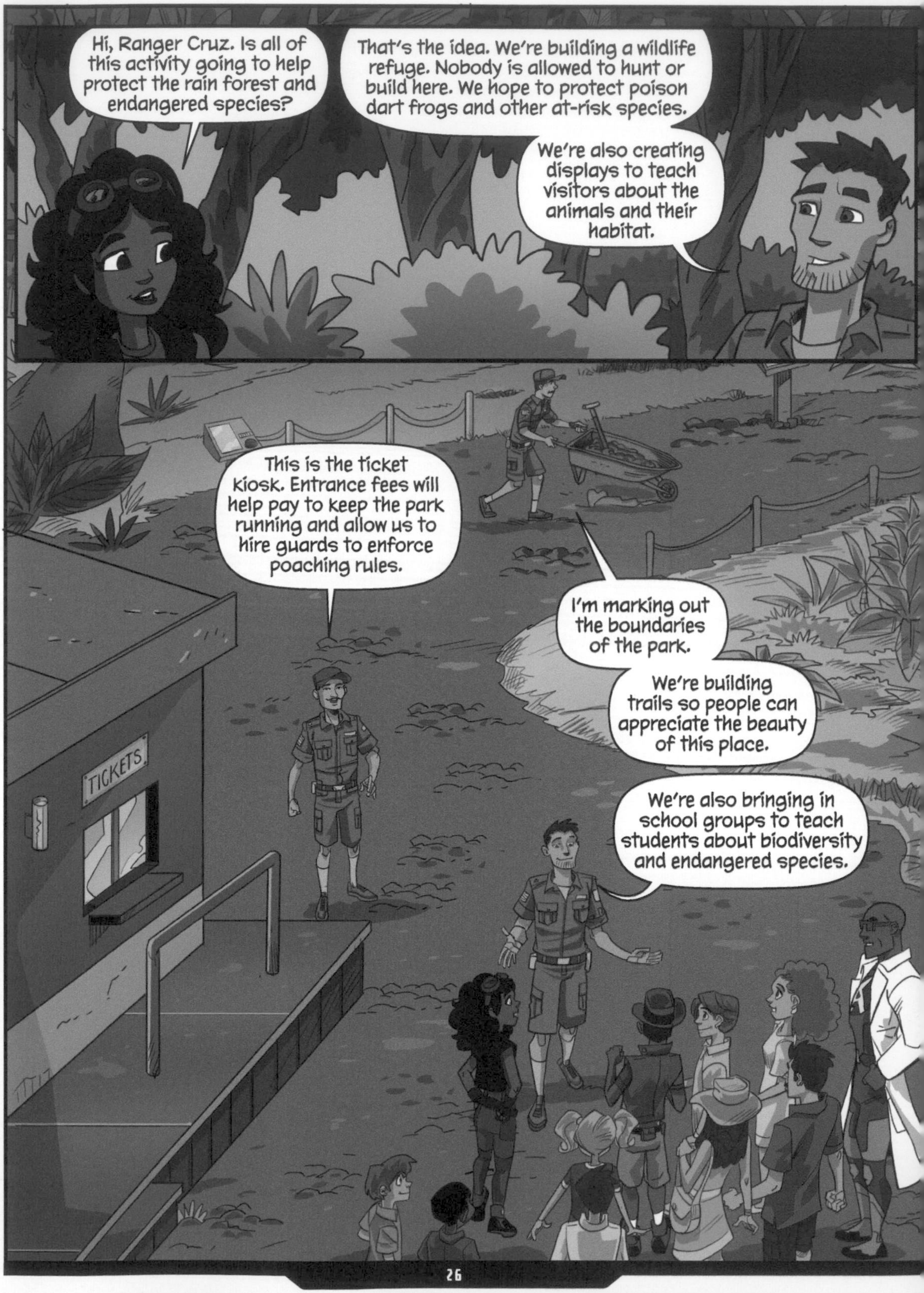
Hi, Ranger Cruz. Is all of this activity going to help protect the rain forest and endangered species?
That's the idea. We're building a wildlife refuge. Nobody is allowed to hunt or build here. We hope to protect poison dart frogs and other at-risk species.
We're also creating displays to teach visitors about the animals and their habitat.
This is the ticket kiosk. Entrance fees will help pay to keep the park running and allow us to hire guards to enforce poaching rules.
I'm marking out the boundaries of the park.
We're building trails so people can appreciate the beauty of this place.
We're also bringing in school groups to teach students about biodiversity and endangered species.
TICKETS

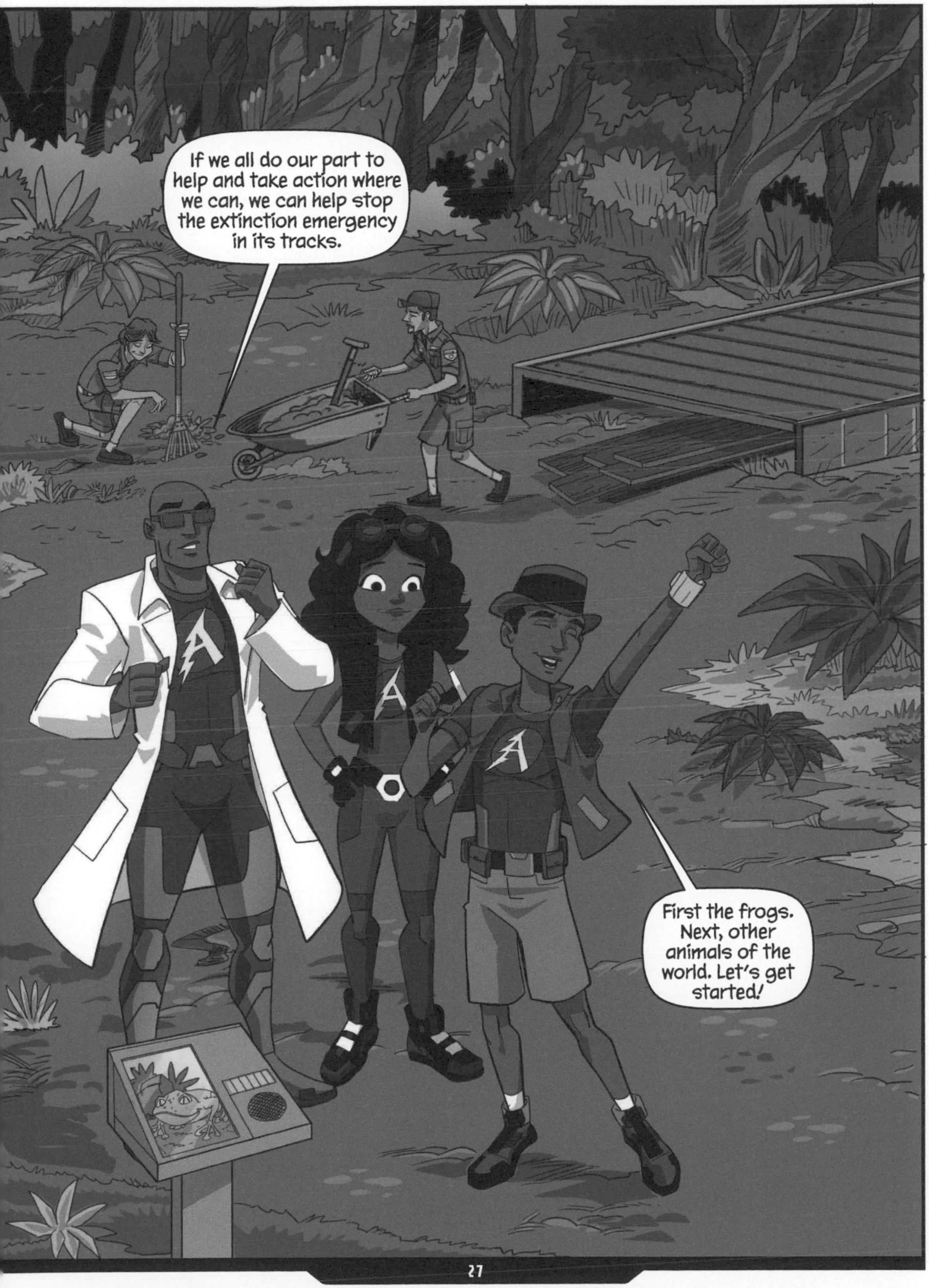
If we all do our part to help and take action where we can, we can help stop the extinction emergency in its tracks.
First the frogs. Next, other animals of the world. Let's get started!

GETTING INVOLVED

Conservation isn't just for adults. There are plenty of ways that kids can learn and take action to protect the many living animals on Earth and their habitats. Check out the list below for different activities and opportunities. Try a few, or get inspired to start something new. Thanks for helping out!

▶ The National Wildlife Federation's Green Hour program offers weekly activities with the goal of getting millions of young people to spend more time in nature. Other programs include wildlife-friendly gardening, tree-planting, and environmental education. *nwf.org/Kids-and-Family/Connecting-Kids-and-Nature*

▶ The Children & Nature Network aims to get kids into nature to make them "healthier, happier and smarter." Young leaders can then make positive changes for the environment. *childrenandnature.org/youth*

▶ Want to protect the oceans? Ask your teacher about becoming an Ocean Guardian Classroom. Through this program by the NOAA National Marine Sanctuaries, schools and classrooms around the world can help protect the oceans. *sanctuaries.noaa.gov/education/og_classroom/welcome.html*

▶ National Geographic offers tips on how to help protect animals all over the world. Find out what actions you can take now. *kids.nationalgeographic.com/explore/nature/save-the-earth-hub/save-animals/*

▶ Earth Rangers' goal is to encourage young conservationists! Through the app, you can get missions to build backyard habitats, protect marine animals, and more. *earthrangers.com*

- Sierra Club: This organization has been getting people out into nature for more than 100 years. Find your local chapter to learn more about outdoor adventures and volunteer activities that families can do together. *sierraclub.org/local-outdoors*

- A lot of volunteer opportunities will be unique to where you live. To find ways to chip in, try contacting local organizations or chapters of national organizations such as:

    - The Audubon Society: *audubon.org*
    - The Nature Conservancy: *nature.org/en-us/get-involved/how-to-help/volunteer-and-attend-events*
    - The Arbor Day Foundation: *arborday.org/trees/treefacts*

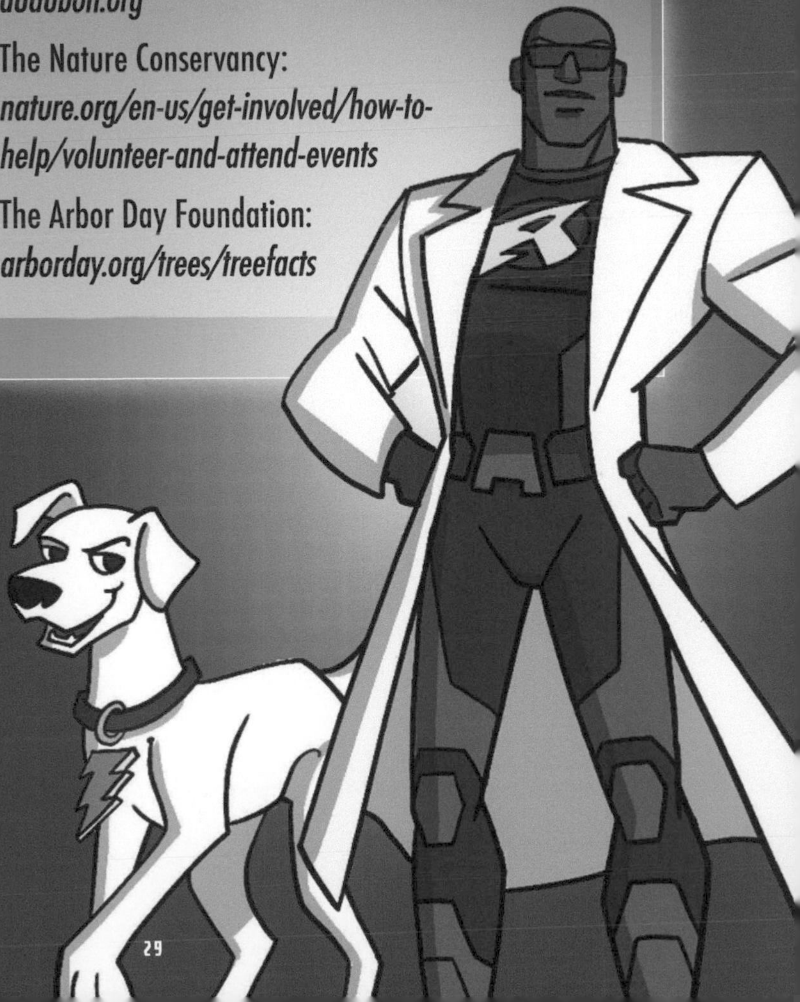

GLOSSARY

biodiversity (bye-oh-duh-VUR-suh-tee)—the number and variety of plants and animals that are found in an area

catastrophic (kat-uh-STROF-ik)—describing a violent and extremely destructive event

conservation (kon-sur-VAY-shuhn)—the protection of earth's natural resources, such as water, forests, and wildlife

endangered (in-DAYN-juhrd)—at risk of dying out and with few individuals left

extinct (ik-STINGKT)—no longer living

habitat (HAB-uh-tat)—the natural place and conditions in which a plant or animal lives

invasive (in-VAY-siv)—not native to an area and may cause harm to the environment into which it was brought

migration (mye-GRAY-shuhn)—the regular movement of animals as they search different places for food

poach (POHCH)—to take a plant or animal from a place where it is illegal to do so

regulations (reg-yuh-LAY-shuhnz)—rules or laws

reproduce (ree-pruh-DOOSE)—to make offspring; many animals reproduce by mating

species (SPEE-sheez)—a group of living things that share common characteristics

READ MORE

Braun, Eric. *Can You Save an Endangered Species? An Interactive Eco Adventure.* North Mankato, MN: Capstone Press, 2021.

Clinton, Chelsea. *Start Now! You Can Make a Difference.* New York: Philomel Books, 2018.

Marotta, Millie. *A Wild Child's Guide to Endangered Animals.* San Francisco: Chronicle Books, 2019.

INTERNET SITES

DK Find Out: Endangered Animals
dkfindout.com/us/more-find-out/special-events/endangered-animals/

Mongabay Rain: Tropical Rain Forest Information for Kids
kids.mongabay.com

U.S. Fish & Widlife: Conservation Kids
fws.gov/international/education-zone/conservation-kids.html

INDEX